School of Divinity

Gardner-Webb University
School of Divinity

This book donated
by

Dr. Herbert Garrett, Jr

A
BETRAYAL OF
INNOCENCE

A

DAVID B. PETERS

BETRAYAL OF INNOCENCE

What Everyone Should Know About Child Sexual Abuse

H
72
.U53
P47
1986

WORD BOOKS
PUBLISHER
WACO, TEXAS

A DIVISION OF
WORD, INCORPORATED

Library of Congress Cataloging-in-Publication Data

Peters, David B., 1946–
   A betrayal of innocence.

   1. Child molesting—United States.   2.   Child molesting—United States—Prevention.   3.   Child molesting—United States—Religious aspects—Christianity.   I.   Title.
HQ72. 453P47   1986   362.7'044   85-26581
ISBN 0-8499-0502-8

Printed in the United States of America

67898 BKC 987654321

I would like to dedicate this book to my loving wife, Lynda, who for eighteen years has been my best friend and source of optimism. Her support, encouragement, and editorial assistance have made the completion of this work possible. Her contribution has been second only to that of our Lord, to whom we are both eternally grateful and committed.

ACKNOWLEDGEMENTS

I would like to gratefully acknowledge the contributions of several people, all of whom played a valuable part in making this book possible. Special thanks to our friends Paul Castle, Charles Stock, Anne Stock, Emile Swift, and Janet Swift for their help in completing the initial manuscripts. Also, Sheri Livingston of Word, Inc. proved to be a most understanding and competent editor during the final stages of manuscript development.

It is with a special sense of kinship that I would like to acknowledge the contributions of my comrades-in-arms, fellow child-protective-service workers Peggy Dutemple, Earlene Keller, and Jan Viss. Over the years, we have shared many frustrations, joys and sorrows while working with abused children and their families. And no list of team members would be complete without mentioning a very special law enforcement officer. Steve Clark, a Sheriff's Investigator in our county's juvenile division, has proven himself to be sensitive and compassionate in dealing with children, even in the most difficult circumstances. I am proud to have had the privilege of working with such dedicated and caring individuals.

And last but not least, I would like to thank all of the victims of sexual abuse who encouraged me to continue this project even when the going got rough, especially those in the victim's support group in our church. They, above all people, are aware of the need for further education on this subject.

CONTENTS

PREFACE

This book contains many examples and illustrations which the reader may, at first, find to be almost unbelievable and certainly emotionally shocking. However, I assure you that the information presented is based entirely on personal experience in investigation and treatment of child sexual abuse and on the best available research material in this field.

Certainly, the sexual abuse of children is an emotional subject which gives rise to strong feelings—especially among Christians, who are admonished to sexual purity. It is understandable that most of us would prefer to dismiss the problem as belonging to a small, depraved segment of our society, but the facts do not allow for such a dismissal.

We are therefore faced with two alternatives: (1) we can ignore the problem and hope that somehow it will not affect us or our loved ones, or (2) we can face the fact of its existence, educate ourselves, act to heal the hurt already inflicted, and try to prevent future damage to untold thousands. I feel confident that if you were able to see the misery and pain in the faces of the hundreds of innocent children and desperate adults with whom I have dealt, there would be no question as to your decision.

Recently there has been a great deal of national publicity in regard to child sexual abuse, both as it occurs within the family and as it is perpetrated by strangers. Accompanying this awareness has been an increase in secular literature on the subject. Expectedly, secular authors seldom consider Scriptural principles when dealing with this subject. Surely the sexual exploitation of our children, whether by strangers or by family members or friends, is a subject of sufficient importance to warrant its study from a Christian perspective.

Since Christians must live in the world, it is imperative that we be aware of the problem of sexual abuse and that we equip ourselves to deal with it in ways which are consistent with our beliefs. To help promote such knowledge and preparation is the desire of my heart and the purpose of this book.

Can we as Christians consider this sensitive subject with open minds and teachable hearts? It is my prayer that the Lord will enable us to do so, and that we use what we learn to help provide protection and healing for ourselves, our families, and the other members of the body of Christ.

CHAPTER ONE

A Message to
Christians

A Case in Point

Judy is devastated. She has just been told that her husband of eight years has been sexually molesting her fourteen-year-old daughter, Cindy, since she was seven years old. Judy is frightened, angry, depressed and confused all at the same time. Whom should she believe? Cindy reported the abuse to a counselor at school and later tearfully pleaded with her mother to believe her. Her husband vehemently denies all the accusations and claims Cindy hates him and just wants to get him out of the home. Judy wants to support her daughter but a panic inside tells her she must believe her husband or lose everything.

In Judy's confusion and pain, it never occurs to her that her daughter's abuse, if it actually did happen, could in any way be related to her own molestation as a child. The fact that she still has regular flashbacks and nightmares about having been molested by her own father doesn't seem to be significant. All she knows is that her world is falling apart.

Judy grew up in a middle-class family in the Sierra Nevada foothills in California. On the outside, her family seemed to be well-adjusted and "normal." Her parents had a stable marriage and the family was actively involved in a local fundamental community church. Although her father might not be considered a committed Christian, he attended church regularly. Her mother was Sunday school superintendent and a faithful worker in the church. Unfortunately, things in this particular family were not as they appeared.

Judy was six when she was first approached sexually by her father. He was self-employed and spent a lot of time at home. Her mother was a nurse and often worked night shifts, which left Judy and her father home alone much of the time. It started with her father getting more and more "loving" while saying "good night" and soon developed into more specific sexual touching. As close as Judy can remember, she was about ten years old when her father first forced her to have intercourse with him. No violence or threats were involved, but it was clear that she had no choice but to submit. Her father claimed he was trying to show her "what mothers and fathers do" to prepare her for her eventual marriage. Judy remembers that first instance well and still cries when she thinks about it. Twenty-eight years have passed, but the pain and confusion are as fresh as if it were yesterday.

Tammy, Judy's little sister, was born when Judy was eleven, and it was not long before Judy was acting as a mother to Tammy. Judy's mother seemed to be around less and less as Judy took on increasing responsibilities in the family. What little relationship her parents had with each other slowly faded to the point of being almost nonexistent, but they stayed together because they did not believe in divorce.

The incidents of sexual abuse became more frequent with the passage of time. By the age of fourteen, Judy was in actuality the mother of her sister and the wife of her father. She felt totally confused and trapped. Praises of "what a grown-up girl you are" from adults offered little in the way of comfort.

Judy thought her mother must have known what was happening. She kept trying to tell her in subtle ways. Several times Judy told her that she didn't like how her father treated her and didn't want to stay home with him all the time. Her mother apparently passed these statements off as the product of teenage rebellion. Judy could not bring herself to talk openly about the molestation because she was afraid it would hurt her mother terribly. Besides, her father often warned her that if she told, the family would fall apart and it would be her fault.

Things remained pretty much unchanged until Judy began to date at the age of sixteen. Her father had refused to let her date before that time and made sure that any boys showing interest in her were quickly put in their place. However, as Judy became more and more interested in boys and saw her friends dating, she pushed harder until her father eventually agreed to limited social activities.

Unfortunately, the only way Judy knew how to relate to males by this time was sexually, and she quickly acquired a reputation as a "bad girl." Her father showed extreme jealousy toward her boyfriends, and tensions continued to mount. After a number of emotional scenes between Judy and her father over a period of two years, she ran away and married one of her boyfriends. Judy was never able to tell her mother about having been abused and did not learn until recently that her father had begun to molest her little sister almost two years before Judy left home.

Now, two husbands and three children later, Judy is reliving the nightmare all over again. She is insecure, considers herself ugly and undesirable with no skills of her own, and is being forced to choose between her husband and her daughter. She has played the role of a victim all of her life, and it does not appear that things are going to change in the foreseeable future.

Everybody's Problem

A pretty far-fetched story? Not at all! This case history describes a family that actually exists. It lists only a small number of the problems created by the molestation. Many items were omitted for the sake of brevity and because, frankly, many people would not believe the story if it were told.

Nor is this an isolated case. Multiplied thousands of families fall prey to such situations in the United States each year. "But surely," you say, "this does not apply to the Christian family. No Christian father or mother would do such a thing to one of their children."

What makes us believe that the same Satan who tempts Christians with fornication, adultery, and homosexuality would hesitate for one moment to use a sin which has the potential of destroying entire Christian families? Indeed, what better weapon against the family could Satan hope for?

When I first began working with victims of sexual abuse and their families, I was shocked to find that most of these families were average, middle-class American families very similar to mine. However, I was smug in the belief that this problem could not *possibly* occur in a truly Christian home. But it wasn't long before I was counseling with several families which seemed to be exceptions to my rule.

In the years since I encountered those first few cases, I have come to believe that Christian families are not only susceptible to this most dangerous problem, but often seem to be primary targets. Counseling with victims and molesters from fundamental Christian families has forced me to recognize that child sexual abuse is a key issue affecting the health of the body of Christ. And along with this reluctant realization has come a sense of urgency on my part for educating Christian families about sexual abuse in the hope of combating its destructive influences on the church.

Whether discussing sexual abuse within a family or at the hands of a stranger, there seems to be a weakness to which we as Christians and as human beings are subject and which exposes us and our loved ones to attack—we desperately want to believe that it will never happen to us. However, for the conscientious Christian, pretending to be immune to this problem is a dangerous gamble with high stakes—the emotional lives of our loved ones. Perhaps the fact that at least one of every four females in the United States is molested by age eighteen will startle us out of complacency if we are tempted to ignore this danger.

Child sexual abuse in our nation cuts across all geographic, cultural, economic, social, and religious boundaries. No matter where we live, who we are, or what we do, we are affected by it in some way. In my work in this field, I have dealt with people from nearly every income range and family background, as well as from almost every denomination and religious group imaginable. All share a common pain and all wish that somehow the problem could have been prevented. We will be looking at many of these families and, hopefully, we can learn from their mistakes.

Our Ignorance—Satan's Advantage

In spiritual as well as physical warfare, surprise is a potent weapon in and of itself. We are warned by God's Word to be sober and vigilant, ready to defend ourselves from Satan's attacks (1 Peter 5:8). In 2 Corinthians 2:11 Paul was able to correctly instruct the Corinthian church in a matter of discipline because he was not ignorant of Satan's devices. In fact, Paul indicates that the Christian's knowledge of Satan's strategy is an effective means of preventing him from gaining an advantage over us. If we are aware of his tools and his designs, we are much less likely to be taken by surprise when he attacks.

Interestingly, the reference given in 2 Corinthians is in regard to discipline administered within the Corinthian church as the result of an incestuous relationship in their midst. It is my sincere belief that our Lord expects us as Christians to be realistic about the existence of such sexual sins and be ready to deal with them rather than ignore them, as the Corinthian church at first had done.

In this book we will discuss proof of the existence of the problem, both from scientific data and from my personal experiences in the investigation and treatment of child sexual abuse. Most discussion will center on child molestation within the family. However, important information will also be given on preventing and treating the sexual abuse of children by those outside the family. We will discuss, in both categories, the effects of child sexual abuse on children and their families, the causes of the abuse, and how to effectively treat the victim and the family. Equally important, we will give specific guidelines on how to recognize that molestation has taken place. This seems especially relevant in light of the fact that only a fraction of the actual occurrences of molestation are ever reported, either to the authorities or the child's parents. Finally, and perhaps most importantly, we will discuss how to prevent sexual abuse in ways which are least traumatic to both child and parent.

In discussing these different aspects of sexual abuse, it is my purpose to speak specifically to three distinct groups of Christians: Christian parents, Christian adults who were molested as children, and Christian counselors. Each of these groups has a specific and important role to play in healing the hurts caused by past sexual abuse and in preventing the victimization of countless other children.

As Christian parents we have a responsibility to be alert to the dangers facing our children, to educate ourselves in prevention, and to be able to recognize and deal with sexual abuse if it does occur. On the other hand, Christian adults who were molested as children are painfully aware of the terrible hurt which accompanies the molestation. However, many do not realize that the problems they are currently facing in their emotional lives, their marriages, and their sexual adjustment are to a great extent the results of being abused as children. As for Christian counselors, most of us have become frustrated with people we are counseling who have multiple and severe problems but do not seem to respond to even the most intense counseling. Often the key to helping such an individual lies in being able to recognize the indicators of previous sexual abuse and treating that client in a way which will promote healing rather than causing further damage. I am confident that the information we are about to cover will prove useful not only to pastors and professional Christian counselors but also to the lay counselor seeking to encourage a fellow believer. We are admonished by the Word to bear one another's burdens (Gal. 6:2). And what better way than by giving encouragement to someone who has been wounded through sexual abuse?

As we discuss this delicate problem more in detail and share in the lives of people who have been affected by it, please keep in mind that the information you need as a concerned individual may be scattered throughout this book. For this reason it is important that you read the entire book before giving advice or making decisions which will affect you, those in your family, and other members of the Body of Christ.

CHAPTER TWO

An Overwhelming Problem

Before discussing such things as the causes, effects, and treatment of child sexual abuse, it must first be established as a problem which affects our lives and the lives of those we love. An extensive review of various statistical studies has been conducted, including the limited material available from Christian sources. I am certain you will find the resulting figures both interesting and disturbing.

In this chapter we also will deal with some common misconceptions and consider the damage done by ignoring sexual abuse or treating it lightly when it's discovered. In addition, we will see why it is so important for us as Christians to educate ourselves in this field, especially those of us to whom the victim might come for help.

Who Hasn't Been?

When I first began speaking to church and community groups about the sexual abuse of children, I was hesitant to use the statistics that had been given to me in different training programs. I had had very little personal experience with such abuse and felt the figures must have been inflated. However, as the years went by and I spent more time investigating and treating these cases, I became painfully aware that the figures given were understatements of the problem.

In talking with mothers and other concerned individuals after speaking engagements, I have been constantly amazed by the number of people who volunteer the fact of their own abuse or that of their children, relatives, and friends. I began asking myself a question heard frequently today among educators on this subject—who *hasn't* been sexually abused? We shall soon see why such a question often seems to be more appropriate than asking who *has* been abused.

Before discussing statistics, let me define child sexual abuse in general and incest in particular. Many different individuals and groups have attempted to define child sexual abuse, and legal definitions differ from state to state. But the National Center on Child Abuse and Neglect has formulated what I consider to be a good definition:

> Contacts or interactions between a child and an adult when the child is being used for the sexual stimulation of the perpetrator or another person. Sexual abuse may also be committed by a person under the age of eighteen when that person is either significantly older than the victim or when the perpetrator is in a position of power or control over another child.

Child sexual abuse as a general category includes both "intrafamilial" and "extrafamilial" sexual abuse. The term *intrafamilial sexual abuse* refers to abuse which takes place within the family. Incest is included in this category and is often referred to using that term. However, there are as many definitions of incest as there are studies and laws on the subject. Many of those definitions, especially legal definitions, require that intercourse must have taken place and that the perpetrator be a close blood relative. However, knowing from experience that extreme psychological damage does not require intercourse and is not dependent on blood relationship, I prefer to define incest as:

> Any type of sexual contact or interaction imposed on a child by a parent, parental figure, sibling, or other family member.

This definition is useful in cases where the abuser is not related to the victim but holds a position of trust and authority over the child. An example of this can be seen in a family we worked with in which an adult male had developed a close relationship with a woman and her three children. He was acting as a community volunteer assigned to help the family adjust within the community. After becoming a "father" to these children, he molested two of them. Because of the molester's position of trust, the damage done to the children was the same as if this had been true incest. Such cases are not at all uncommon.

Extrafamilial sexual abuse usually describes sexual abuse of a child by a molester not related to the victim. This is the type of molestation we hear about so often in the news media, but sexual abuse by strangers is much less common than abuse by persons known and trusted by the victims. For instance, in a study done recently at the Harborview Medical Center-Sexual Assault Center in Seattle, Washington, statistics were collected on nearly six hundred children seen by the center during a twenty-one-month period. Eighty-five percent of these victims were female and 62 percent were less than twelve years of age. Eighty percent were white, 10 percent black, and the remainder belonged to various minority groups. The offender was male in 90 percent of the cases.

Perhaps the most important figure to be aware of in this study is that in only 8 percent of these cases was the offender a stranger to the child. Forty-seven percent or nearly half of the offenders were family members, and most of the other offenders were people known to the victim. Only in a small percentage of these cases was a stranger the perpetrator of sexual abuse, yet it is the stranger who is generally targeted by the media.[1]

Time and space limitations do not permit a complete summary of all the surveys and reports reviewed. Consequently, we will only cover information from several of the most recent and representative reports. These figures reflect findings from across the nation and are really on the conservative end of the spectrum.

Many of the current studies are restricted to certain selected populations and so are not always applicable to the general public. Some of the most widely quoted works—including such studies as those done by Landis in 1940 and 1956, by Kinsey in 1953, and by Cagnon and Finkelhor in 1965 and 1978—were done mainly on middle-class populations. However, recent studies on more representative populations show that the prevalence and effects of child sexual abuse are very similar, regardless of social class, economic status, or racial background.[2]

Statistically, the sexual abuse of female children is much more common than that of males. In fact, until recently the sexual abuse of boys was virtually ignored. But studies have indicated that male sexual abuse is much more common than previously realized. The dynamics of male sexual abuse will be discussed in detail in chapter 7, which is devoted entirely to that subject. However, to use both "he" and "she" in every appropriate instance is both confusing and cumbersome. So, for clarity and consistency, we have generally used feminine pronouns when referring to victims. In addition, as molesters are almost always male, masculine pronouns are used in this reference. No discrimination is intended.

Regarding the sexual abuse of female children, perhaps the most representative study to date was that conducted by Diana Russell, Professor of Sociology at Mills College in Oakland, California. In that study, trained researchers interviewed a random sample of 930 women from the population at large.

Russell reported that when both categories of sexual abuse (intrafamilial and extrafamilial) were combined, a total of 38 percent of the women surveyed indicated they had been molested before the age of eighteen, and 28 percent said they had been molested before the age of fourteen. When "unwanted non-contact sexual experiences" volunteered by those interviewed were added to these figures, fully 54 percent of the women surveyed claimed to have experienced sexual abuse either inside or outside the family before the age of eighteen. Forty-eight percent reported having had such an experience before the age of fourteen.[3] Unwanted non-contact sexual experiences include such actions as genital exposure, non-genital touch, and sexual advances made by an adult but not acted upon.

In 1979, a study done by Edward Sarafino projected that there may be 336,000 children or more molested in our nation each year.[4] However, even such shocking figures seem to be gross understatements when considering recent material available from studies such as Russell's. Is it any wonder that those of us working in this field are beginning to ask, "Who *hasn't* been sexually abused?"

When considering the information now available in this field, the average individual is tempted to pretend that this problem does not apply to him. Surely it belongs to people in another area, of another lifestyle, holding different beliefs. Christians are not immune to these rationalizations. However, we must realize that we have a unique opportunity to be in the vanguard of prevention and treatment efforts in this field. Many of these families will seek help from their spiritual advisors when they will not from a secular society. Thus, we find ourselves in a position of opportunity and grave responsibility.

Students at the Graduate School of Psychology at Fuller Theological Seminary recently conducted a survey of pastors and Christian counselors on the subject of incest. Their findings reflect some of the concerns and challenges which this topic presents to the Christian community. Fifty-five pastors and 112 counselors responded to the questionnaires sent out and reported having worked with 981 cases of incest in their counseling experience.

The general characteristics reported by these pastors and counselors seemed basically to fit the study profile seen in secular findings. Ninety percent of the reported victims were female. Fathers and stepfathers were the most common offenders (48 percent as reported by pastors, 56 percent as reported by counselors). Fathers were more often the abusers than were stepfathers. In 64 percent of these cases, the incest began when the child was between seven and thirteen years of age. Incest cases reported seldom involved single incidents of molestation. Sixty percent of the cases reported by the pastors and 65 percent of those reported by the counselors were repeated incidents spanning a year or more. In nearly half of the cases reported by Christian counselors, it was believed that more than one child in the family had been molested. It was also estimated by the pastors that 62 percent of their incest families were "middle or upper class," while the counselors estimated that 66 percent of their clients fell within that category.[5] Such figures make it difficult for us to follow our natural inclination to deny that child sexual abuse affects Christians in this day and age.

Those working with the problem of child sexual abuse in the Christian community are becoming more and more aware of the immensity of this problem. They are also aware, as are secular counselors, of the need for training in the dynamics and treatment of sexual abuse and in the tools available for its prevention. Almost all of those who responded to the questionnaires in the Fuller study felt the need for workshops, open discussions, literature, and educational material for themselves and others in dealing with this problem. Along with this realization of need has come a promise of opportunity and hope.

These same pastors and counselors who reflected feelings of helplessness in the face of this problem also volunteered the thought that the Christian community has the unique opportunity of introducing healing in these families through forgiveness, acceptance, and love for all involved. In most of the cases reported in this study, the victims had not counseled with anyone previous to their request for pastoral counseling. Because of this, it is imperative that the Christian community educate itself about child sexual abuse. The need is indeed overwhelming!

Dispelling Some Myths

Before we can get on with the business of considering the effects of child sexual abuse and what can be done about it, we would do well to dispel a few of the myths held by the general public in regard to this problem. We have already dealt with some in this chapter.

First, we learned that child sexual abuse, both within and outside of the family, is a huge and increasing problem in America. We also learned that most molesters are not strangers but are people known and often trusted by the victim. We saw that sexual abuse does not occur mainly among minorities, the poor, or the uneducated. The average American family can be and is very much affected by the problem. We further learned that the Christian family is by no means free from the dangers of sexual abuse in any of its forms.

Other misconceptions I have encountered regularly while speaking on this subject have equal potential for harm. One such myth is the idea that molesters are violent. In the vast majority of cases within or outside of the family, no violence whatsoever is used. In fact, the relationship between molester and victim often appears at first to be close and supportive. Only later is the extent of the damage done by such "innocent" relationships seen for what it is.

Another misconception is that molesters tend to be mentally ill and to exhibit bizarre behavior. Again, group profiling of molesters indicates that less than 10 percent are classifiable as "mentally ill." Most are immature, socially inadequate individuals who outwardly appear normal. This myth is hard to erase because people want to believe the molester is a mentally deranged monster to avoid facing the fact that he could be a family member or friend. I never cease to be amazed by the throngs of people who turn out to supply emotional and even financial support to molesters brought to trial. "Obviously," the community says, "he can't be a molester. He's a fine, upstanding citizen." This phenomenon is intensified by the fact that these men are often scout leaders, teachers, church youth group workers, and respected professionals—including officers of the law, doctors, and attorneys. Our society has much to learn about outward appearances. This should be no surprise to Christians in light of 1 Samuel 16:7, which states that "man looks on the outward appearance, but the LORD looks on the heart."

A further example of our desperation to ignore the sexual abuse of children is the totally erroneous statement often heard: "It may not be true. After all, children lie about many things and could fantasize about having been sexually abused." Of all the cases I have investigated and seen investigated, I know of only one instance of a child lying about sexual abuse. Furthermore, every authority in the nation as far as I am aware reports the same conclusion. Children have neither the inclination nor the information necessary for false reporting. Also, children may lie to get out of trouble, but they seldom lie to get into it. And believe me, children know that reporting sexual abuse will cause trouble.

- Equally ludicrous in the mythology of this subject is the statement that some children enjoy sexual activity with adults and encourage it by being seductive. Children are naturally affectionate and, unlike adults, are not inhibited in their expression of affection. Some adults interpret this as a "come-on." They assume that the child is asking for sexual interaction when all she really wants is to be hugged and cuddled. The claim that these children are consciously asking to be molested is a product of the perverse mind of an adult seeking to rationalize the abuse of children. This is an excuse we hear over and over again from molesters: "She was asking for it so I gave it to her." How deceitful and desperately wicked is the heart of man (Jer. 17:9). Let me assure any would-be rationalizers reading this book that your child is asking for physical attention—not sex. It is your responsibility as an adult to refrain from presuming upon the innocence of any child.

There are numerous other myths regarding sexual abuse that we will be unable to cover here. Many of these relate to the treatment and prevention of sexual abuse and will be dealt with in later chapters. It is hoped that the others will be dispelled as we make progress in this book.

Healing Lightly

Hopefully, many of you as readers are now convinced of the prevalence of child sexual abuse and the fact that it can influence you and those you love. Parents, especially Christians, must be made aware that there is another danger which presents itself. This danger is the tendency of the parent, pastor, Christian counselor, or relative of the victim to deny that abuse occurred or to underestimate the damage done by the acts of molestation. Such rationalization on the part of concerned adults is certainly understandable, but it can have a disastrous effect on the victim of sexual abuse. In many cases it encourages continued molestation of the child, often prolonging her emotional torture for years.

Both secular and Christian counselors dealing with such cases often suffer from a serious lack of training in this field, and so they make decisions that adversely affect the lives of thousands of children each year. They often assume that the reported sexual abuse consisted of isolated incidents or, at worst, was a mistake made by the molester in a moment of weakness or a particularly difficult time in his life. In incest cases especially, even highly trained professionals are often quick to gloss over the damage caused to the victim and to return the child to the environment which spawned the abuse in the first place. They even use the confused emotions of the child to justify returning the molester to the home without realizing they are condemning the victim and possibly other children in the home to further abuse. Following is an excerpt from a letter written by a psychiatrist to the superior court in regard to a family with which we counseled:

> I am writing you regarding the requested psychiatric approval for Mr. K. to return home to live. I saw him for a follow-up appointment on July 1, at which time he appraised me of the events since he had last been seen in April, events which obviously had been rather traumatic for him. . . . He has had no further fallout in terms of relating to his stepchildren. They have all been very supportive, as have all of his friends. This has been an unusual situation, certainly the kind of situation which probably suggests a potential very happy ending, as he is basically a very stable person for whom the kinds of activities he carried on would be considered very unusual. Probably he carried on such sexual activities because he had never been caught and had developed some bad habits. Now that he has finally been caught it has been given him in no uncertain terms that in the future, were this ever to happen, there would be major consequences. I don't feel that a great deal of psychotherapy or counseling will be required. I do feel that to be monitored on a regular basis should still be considered. I have suggested seeing him again in three or four months after he returns home, probably six months after that, probably annually after that. I will certainly be available for additional appointments if situations warrant it. At the present time I see no evidence of any mental illness, no evidence of sexual preoccupations. Therefore, it is more than psychiatrically all right for him to return to his home as quickly as possible.
>
> Sincerely, Dr. M., M.D.

The stepfather in this family had assumed the psychological role of father to these three girls. It was learned that this man was sexually molesting two of his stepdaughters and had been doing so for quite some time. The abuse came to the attention of the authorities indirectly and he was arrested and removed from the home. During criminal proceedings the court ordered him evaluated by a psychiatrist. The evaluation was completed as seen above and, as a result, this man was allowed to return home. Surely, everyone thought, in view of the "major consequences" mentioned by the psychiatrist, this man would not remolest. And, after all, he was a "stable person."

For her part, the mother of the girls was careful not to leave the girls alone with her husband. However, one day the eight-year-old girl who had not been molested stayed home from school because of illness. Her mother had to go to the store and assumed that surely nothing would happen in the short time she was gone. During those few minutes, her husband molested the third daughter.

This molester was charged with another count of molestation and was eventually sent to a state prison, where he remains today. But at what price did this family and our legal system learn a lesson? A child has been molested and emotionally scarred without reason. This molestation was the direct result of a lack of training and knowledge on the part of the psychiatrist, the judge, and the girl's mother. Parents, counselors, judges, attorneys, pastors, and the public at large must be educated about the problem of sexual abuse in order that this story will not be repeated countless times across our nation.

Even after such cases come to light and are referred to counseling, there often is one grave injustice after another. Uninformed counselors discount the damage done to the child, often dismissing the victim with "she'll get over it" or "she's a child and children are very resilient." Christian counselors confronted with an adult who was molested as a child may advise her simply to "forgive" the molester and "get on with her life," or advise a young victim to stay away from her father and tell her mother if it happens again. An uninformed counselor is worse than no counselor at all when it comes to sexual abuse. Professionals trying to help without having had any background in this area have contributed to the destruction of countless emotional lives.

We Christians would do well to take stock of our own attitudes toward this problem. The nonchalant attitude of the inhabitants of Jerusalem was rebuked by Jeremiah the prophet,

"They have healed the wound of my people lightly,
saying, 'Peace, peace,'
when there is no peace" (Jer. 6:14).

Let us pray that this will not be said of us.

Child sexual abuse is a wound not easily dismissed or healed. Above all people, Christians have a unique opportunity to help heal in truth. However, this can only be accomplished through an honest look at the problem and possible solutions. We need to realize that sexual abuse affects Christians and non-Christians alike and place ourselves in the battle to defeat this terrible enemy. As we gain knowledge, we are held responsible by God to use it to maximum advantage.

CHAPTER THREE

Why Us?

Now that we have been made acutely aware of the reality and scope of this problem, it is important that we also consider some of the factors that contribute to it.

As in any other area of human behavior, the reasons for child sexual abuse are multiple and complex. We cannot simply attribute this problem to spiritual shortcomings, or blame it all on the devil. Neither can we classify it as purely a psychological or sociological problem, or attribute it to the upbringing of the molester. Ultimately, the sole responsibility for these inexcusable acts rests totally on the shoulders of the molester. He, as the adult, is responsible for exercising self-control and deciding against taking sexual advantage of a child.

There is very little scientific data available at this point on the factors that cause sexual abuse. While we may speculate on some of the reasons for it, the hard evidence is not yet in. We will discuss in this chapter factors that seem to be prevalent in many of these cases. We will also review specific examples which seem to bear out some of the suspicions of those of us working with this problem. It is at least encouraging that most experts in this field seem to agree on many of the basic elements contributing to child sexual abuse. They see a common thread running through these families and, while the scientific evidence is not conclusive, it is convincing enough for us to start waving some warning flags.

The main area in which I personally differ with many others reporting on this problem is the influence that spiritual factors may have in causing abuse. As may be expected, secular authorities give little, if any, consideration to the spiritual aspects of this problem, let alone any thought to the possibility that the Bible might have some light to shed on this subject. My personal conviction is that the Bible does indeed have some valuable information to share and that it is necessary for us to consider the spiritual as well as the social and psychological factors when looking for the causes of this problem.

The Bible does not contain much direct commentary on the subject of child sexual abuse. However, it does deal specifically with the subject of incest and gives us some general guidelines on the place children hold in the heart of God. As in any other area of life, there are those in both the secular and the Christian community who ignore the biblical commentary on this subject or twist it to suit their needs.

I recently attended a training seminar on child sexual abuse to which hundreds of professionals had come to learn more about this problem. At the beginning of the seminar, one of the key speakers made an interesting comment. She implied that even God didn't seem to care about the victims of father-daughter incest since, in chapter 18 of the book of Leviticus, the Bible does not specifically prohibit sexual contact with one's own daughter. She began with verse 7 of chapter 18 and read part of the list of persons with whom Hebrew men were commanded not to have any sexual contact. Those listed include his father, mother, stepmother, sister, granddaughter, stepsister, aunt, uncle, daughter-in-law, and sister-in-law, to name a few. Daughters were not specifically named in this list. The omission of any specific reference to daughters seemed to convince the speaker that the Bible somehow supports the idea of daughters being the property of their fathers to do with as they choose, even to the extent of involving them in an incestuous relationship.

At the other end of the spectrum is an incest family with which I came in contact not long ago. The father in this family described himself as a fundamental Christian and was actively involved in "the ministry." He had begun molesting both of his daughters when they were very young. This molestation had continued with one of the daughters for more than twenty years. In talking to her, I learned that just before each incident of molestation, her father would take out his Bible and read to her from Leviticus, chapter 18. He would explain that since daughters were not excluded in the Bible from sexual activity with their fathers, it was all right for them to have sexual contact.

What is interesting in both of these cases is that the conference speaker and the molester alike began their Scripture recital at verse 7 of chapter 18. Had they begun one verse earlier in the text, they would have revealed the true mind of God. "None of you shall approach to any one near of kin to him to uncover nakedness. I am the LORD" (Lev. 18:6). Quoting Scripture out of context is nothing new. But doing so to blame God for passive support of incest or to gain a tool for victimizing one of his little ones provides us with two glaring examples of the deceptiveness of man's heart.

As we review biblical principles that have a bearing on the causes of child sexual abuse, it is my prayer that those who may have a tendency to attribute the problem totally to social and psychological factors will become aware of the spiritual aspects of this subject. Conversely, it is my hope that those of us who tend to spiritualize everything will realize that there are social and psychological factors involved in this problem and that by being aware of them, we can better prepare ourselves and our children to prevent sexual abuse.

The World, the Flesh, and the Devil

The World: The Bible tells us that we as Christians are not of the world because Christ has chosen us out of the world (John 15:19). That is, we do not belong to the world system. However, the Scriptures are equally clear that God has planned for us to be in the world. In John 18:18, Jesus stated that he has sent us into the world just as the Father had sent him.

While Christians are admonished to avoid being "conformed to this world" (Rom. 12:2) and warned in numerous instances to avoid its influences, few of us would deny that the world does indeed tend to influence us. Obviously, the effects of the world system on the non-Christian are even more serious since, by biblical definition, the unbeliever is of the world and usually seeks to embrace rather than to avoid its influences.

The world affects both Christians and non-Christians in a number of different ways. Entertainment, advertising, peer pressures, educational systems, and prevailing philosophies are only a few of the influences affecting the beliefs and behaviors of people. Under the guise of fulfillment, freedom of the press, and humanistic pursuit of happiness, society allows the moral climate to become relative. As a result, victimization of those less able to defend themselves becomes increasingly possible. Unfortunately, the group most susceptible to such victimization in our society is our children.

People often ask me when I speak to various groups, "Do you think sexual abuse of children is on the increase, or that it is simply being reported more?" I have to answer that I feel it is a little of both. There is no question that the number of reports has increased dramatically in the past few years and that public education on the subject is having a positive effect on that trend. However, the more I consider this question, the more I am convinced that child sexual abuse is increasing in our nation. There is a mounting consensus among professionals, especially those treating more serious sex offenders, that child sexual abuse is indeed increasing, and that child pornography is at least partially to blame for that increase.

Child pornography in our nation is a problem of epidemic proportions. It is, I believe, both a cause and a result of the increase in child sexual abuse. Most professionals I have spoken with who are directly involved in treating the more "hard core" child molesters agree. They state categorically that pornography contributes to the molester's problems and lowers his inhibitions. They also report that the more a molester is exposed to child pornography, the coarser and more violent the pornographic material has to be to produce sexual excitement. This phenomenon of moral deadening of the senses is seen in many of Satan's other devices, such as alcoholism and drug addiction. Also, the market for pornography is an indirect result of child sexual abuse. Without people interested in purchasing indecent pictures of children, there would be no market for the product and much less reason for children to be tricked and forced into participating in such activities.

A more measurable indicator of increased sexual abuse of children is the fact that venereal disease in young children seems to be on the increase in our society. I was shocked to read in a recent newspaper article that the number of gonorrhea cases among children under ten years old increased by almost 94 percent in California between 1981 and 1983. I was equally shocked to learn from this article that nearly half of the sexually abused children seen at the University of California Medical Center in Sacramento are aged five or younger. Such figures are a frightening commentary on the direction our nation is taking in this area.

Another disturbing development indicative of our relative morality in this nation is the tremendous increase in the use of children in sexually provocative advertisements. A society which allows its children to be used in such a way on the one hand and cries in agony over the sexual abuse of thousands of its children on the other is caught in a serious moral dilemma. It is my personal opinion that even now there is being waged in the conscience of our nation a terrible battle. Incest, commonly referred to as the "last taboo," and child sexual abuse in general are being weighed on the moral balances.

This same process took place not many years ago in regard to homosexuality in our society. The results of the decision made in that case are obvious today. However, there is a very important distinction to be made when comparing that decision with the one we now face in regard to child sexual abuse. The Bible tells us that in regard to homosexuality, God "gave them up to dishonorable passions" with the result that they received "in their own persons the due penalty for their error" (Rom. 1:26-27). In the case of homosexuality, the harm is done between those consenting to such acts. In the sexual abuse of children, the damage is done to innocent victims incapable of consent.

Our nation should be reminded of the warning Christ gave concerning children. As he placed a small child in the midst of the disciples he stated,

> Whoever receives one such child in my name receives me; but whoever causes one of these little ones who believe in me to sin, it would be better for him to have a great millstone fastened round his neck and to be drowned in the depth of the sea (Matt. 18:5-6).

Let us pray that society makes the right decision in this moral battle. Though I do not consider myself a prophet of doom, I can foresee nothing but judgment ahead for a nation which would choose to abandon its children to such abuse.

The Flesh: The world's influence on the incidence of child sexual abuse is not the only spiritual factor to be considered when discussing possible causes. Another important element is the internal influence which the flesh and lust have on human moral choices. This influence originates within each individual, as opposed to the influence of the world, which is an external force resulting from the environment in which we live. Put simply, the world and the devil are the enemies without, the flesh and lust are the enemies within.

In his letter to the Romans, the apostle Paul explains to us that we as Christians are not in the flesh, but in the Spirit because we have the Spirit of Christ (Rom. 8:9). However, as most Christians are aware, we do not always walk after the Spirit and are not always spiritually minded as is the ideal for Christians set forth in Romans 8:4-6. If we were, there would be no need for the numerous admonitions to holiness we find throughout the

New Testament, including that found later in Romans where Paul tells the Roman Christians,

> But put ye on the Lord Jesus Christ, and make not provision for the flesh, to fulfil the lusts thereof (Rom. 13:14, KJV).

Wherever the flesh is found, lust seems to be close at hand. And lust, as seen in many Scriptures, breeds sin and death. The Bible tells us in James 1:14–15 that

> every man is tempted, when he is drawn away of his own lust, and enticed. Then when lust hath conceived, it bringeth forth sin: and sin, when it is finished, bringeth forth death (KJV).

There dwells within every individual, Christian and non-Christian alike, a tendency to desire what has been forbidden. Lust is a hard thing to defeat, even if we are so inclined. And the non-Christian has no real reason to put up a fight against it.

Christians, however, are admonished by Paul to

> put off your old nature which belongs to your former manner of life and is corrupt through deceitful lusts, and be renewed in the spirit of your minds, and put on the new nature, created after the likeness of God in true righteousness and holiness (Eph. 4:22–24).

Unfortunately, we as Christians often fail in our attempts to put off our old natures, and non-Christians are encouraged by the world system to enjoy those natures. The result is that Christian and non-Christian alike sin in many areas of their lives.

Child sexual abuse is only one of the areas in which this tendency finds its expression. We must be honest with ourselves and others about the possibility of such sins occurring among Christians as well as among non-Christians. Honesty is the first step in arming ourselves to deal with the problem head-on.

The Devil: We have already discussed Satan's desire to destroy the family unit and his use of child sexual abuse in his attempt to accomplish that end. I have no question at all about this being his aim. Although Satan gets a lot of help from our flesh and the natural inclination of our fallen natures toward lust, he is not one to take chances. He is actively involved in orchestrating situations within the world system to meet his needs.

The Word of God makes it clear that the "course of this world" is controlled by the "prince of the power of the air" (Eph. 2:2). He is described elsewhere in the Bible as "the god of this world" who has "blinded the minds of the unbelievers" (2 Cor. 4:4). Satan has been working against the best interests of mankind since he approached Eve in the garden. His purposes are still the same. He comes only to "steal and kill and destroy" (John 10:10). The world system is designed by him to accomplish those purposes, and the sexual abuse of children appears to be one of his most effective tools.

Those individuals of the world who are courageous enough to fight the evil of child sexual abuse seek to do so with laws, regulations, and education. While these weapons can and should be utilized in the fight against this problem, there is a dimension sadly lacking in their battle plan. Once we understand that Satan plays a big part in the opposition, we must begin to use weapons that are effective against him. Paul wrote to the Corinthians that "though we live in the world we are not carrying on a worldly war, for the weapons of our warfare are not worldly but have divine power to destroy strongholds" (2 Cor. 10:3-4). Spiritual weapons are essential when fighting a spiritual enemy. So, along with legal and educational weapons, let us as Christians take up the spiritual weapons of prayer and the Word of God, without which the battle will surely be lost.

Uninformed Parents

While there are most definitely spiritual factors contributing to the incidence of sexual abuse of children, it is also important to realize that there are a number of other factors that must be considered in order to understand and prevent this problem. One of the most important of these factors is the lack of information that parents have in several crucial areas. Those of us trained in this field are constantly amazed by parents who set their children up for sexual abuse without even being aware of it. Unfortunately, what is obvious to us because of our involvement in this field has never occurred to these parents.

The first area I would like to discuss in this context is the difference in sexual response and behavior between males and females. It is crucial for parents to understand, especially in choosing caretakers for their children, that there is a basic and undeniable difference between male and female in the areas of sexual drive, sexual stimuli response, and inclination to act out sexual fantasies. The Word of God tells us that while spiritually there is no distinction in the eyes of God between male and female (Gal. 3:28), biologically, they were created as separate and distinct beings (Gen. 1:27).

Most family counselors will tell you that both men and women have great difficulty in understanding the sexual response or lack of response in their partners. It seems impossible for either partner to understand what makes their mate "tick" sexually. Again, this is due primarily to the fact that they were created as different creatures. My wife can understand intellectually why I respond differently than she. However, she cannot fully understand what I am explaining to her because she is not a man. The same holds true in regard to my understanding of her sexual makeup.

In the next few paragraphs, I will attempt a quick summary of the basic differences in sexual response between men and women. An understanding of these differences is crucial to our ability to protect our children. It is my considered opinion that a large percentage of the cases of child sexual abuse in our nation could have been avoided if parents had believed and acted upon what I am about to explain to you. Please keep in mind that these are general sexual characteristics and in certain areas may not apply to every individual.

Males, as a general rule, tend to have an immediate and strong sexual response to visual stimulation. In other words, they become immediately sexually aroused by merely looking at a sexually appealing object. The personality, character, or intelligence of the individual residing within the body being admired seems to be of little importance, at least in regard to initial sexual response. Men are also more likely than women to act quickly on any fantasies resulting from sexual excitement. While a woman may need the right environment, circumstances, and emotional support for a satisfying sexual experience, such preliminaries are much less important to men. Simply put, men tend to be more sexually volatile and to act more quickly on their sexual desires.

Females, on the other hand, tend to respond less to visual stimulation than to tactile stimulation (touch). They are sexually aroused by kissing, gentle caressing, and other expressions of care and gentleness. They also are more concerned about the character and personality of the individual they are attracted to than are men and consequently are more likely to respond sexually to someone they respect and feel safe with.

Few people are really aware of the differences in sexual response just related. Consequently, this information is seldom considered when making decisions on child care and employment scheduling. It is my opinion that ignorance of this subject is one of the main direct causes of child sexual abuse.

A common problem we deal with in the field of sexual abuse is the parent or parents who arrange for a caretaker without consideration to the sex of the caretaker, the presence of another responsible adult, or the background and problems the caretaker may have. For example, putting a teenage boy in the position of baby-sitting female children is not only dangerous for the children, but is unfair to the boy. How many mothers I have heard exclaim in righteous indignation, "He could never have done anything like that. He's a good boy." Again, they do not understand the differences in sexual response between males and females and the added problems of a teenage boy feeling the pressures of sexual awakening. Parents, and especially mothers, need to be aware of these basic differences, whether the proposed caretaker is a boy or a man.

I recently read a newspaper article regarding the conviction of a local man on charges of sexually molesting two young girls. The parents had allowed this man to baby-sit their daughters on numerous occasions and had even allowed them to stay overnight at his house several times. The fact that this individual is married and has children of his own may have given these parents a false sense of security. The point is that we as parents cannot be too careful when making decisions regarding caretakers for our children. Above all, we must keep in mind the differences in sexual response we have just discussed.

Before leaving the topic of uninformed parents, we should at least touch on a subject having a very real impact on the problem of inappropriate caretakers. "The pursuit of happiness" is a phrase near and dear to the heart of our nation. While our right to the pursuit of happiness is guaranteed to every citizen by the Bill of Rights, it appears that its extreme application by some parents contributes to the likelihood that their children will become the victims of child sexual abuse.

It has become so important for each individual in our society to achieve "personal fulfillment" that we go to great lengths to overcome any obstacles to that goal. If both parents have to work long and irregular hours in order to improve the family lifestyle or augment the family possessions, this is considered a necessity. If something less than ideal child care arrangements are available, perhaps this can be overlooked for the sake of pursuing "happiness." In the course of such pursuits, our children are often shortchanged in affection and family interaction. Also, they are often subjected to questionable child care providers because there was no alternative. Often the simplest checks of child care suitability are neglected. Excuses of "it can't be helped" are of little comfort to children molested by a caretaker. For them, this all-consuming pursuit of happiness becomes a right guaranteed only to adults.

The final point I would like to discuss in considering uninformed parents is the part that inappropriate sleeping arrangements can play in contributing to child sexual abuse. Obviously, this subject has more of a bearing on incestuous abuse than on extrafamilial abuse. While often overlooked when considering causes of sexual abuse, the existence of inappropriate sleeping arrangements in families seems to be exposed quite frequently in our investigation of incest cases.

Psychologists and psychiatrists seem generally to agree that allowing children of different sexes to share a room or allowing a child to share the bed of a parent or parents can be psychologically damaging to children. Dr. Gabriel Laury, Associate Professor of Clinical Psychiatry at State University of New York at Stony Brook, states that "faulty sleeping arrangements can represent a subtle form of sexual abuse." He points out that allowing children to share a room or bed with a sibling of the opposite sex or with a parent can be harmful to the child's psychosexual development. In the case of siblings, such arrangements can lead to "continuous premature sexual overstimulation and unhealthy sexual games, which may be followed by gnawing guilt and anxiety in the children."[6]

In sharing a room or bed with a parent or parents, a child may be exposed to sexual activity without the information needed to properly interpret that activity. In such cases, children often misinterpret sexual interaction between parents as violence or fighting. Or, they may become sexually stimulated long before it is socially acceptable for them to act out what they have learned. In either case, a child's reaction to such exposure can result in psychological problems for the child and embarrassing social problems for the parents.

In the case of a child sleeping with one parent in the absence of the other, such arrangements can and often do lead to incestuous sexual activity. These situations rarely start with any intent on the part of the adult to molest the child. However, to place one sexually experienced human being in extended and close contact with the unclothed or partially clothed body of another human being is asking for trouble. This is especially true when a female child is sleeping with an adult male. Additionally, when you combine the "chemical" sexual responses of the human body with loneliness, emotional immaturity, or inhibition relaxers such as alcohol, the mixture is even more explosive.

While the effects of such arrangements on a child are admittedly influenced by the age and sex of the child, the sex of the parent, and various other factors, it is a good general rule not to take such a chance in the first place. We would do well to heed the admonition of the Scriptures to "abstain from all appearance of evil" (1 Thes. 5:22, KJV). If we have any question at all about how such behavior will affect our children, we should avoid it completely.

Ideally, children should never be allowed to develop the habit of sleeping with their parents, even when young. If such a habit has already been established, it should be broken as soon as possible. Simple measures such as reading to a child before bed and not allowing any viewing of violent television programs just prior to bedtime can be effective in preventing the fears that may initially send children to the bed of their parents.

The warnings and concerns I have been relating may be interpreted by some as paranoia or at the very least an overreaction to a minor problem. However, I assure you that there is a basis for concern in this area. Even now I am reminded of one young girl previously in our treatment program who expressed a particularly strong hatred of her natural father, who was also in our program. When this girl was seven years old, she had been frightened one night during a lightning storm and had run to her parents' bedroom for comfort. This was not an unusual occurrence in their family, but it so happened that this particular night her mother was working and her father was alone in bed. Her father claims that when she snuggled close to him in fear, he misinterpreted her actions, became sexually excited and began to fondle her. That incident began a period of sexual abuse lasting years, which destroyed the love once held between father and daughter and left a legacy of bitter hatred.

The fault in this incident and in every incident of child sexual abuse lies squarely at the feet of the molester. However, one cannot help but wonder if this story would have been different had that girl not gotten in the habit of running to the bed of her parents when frightened. Again, we as parents need to take every precaution possible to decrease the chance of our children being sexually abused. If we dismiss some of these factors as being petty or not applicable to our family, they may very well come back to haunt us.

Blind Obedience

A common message to children in the average American family is that they should always obey adults. This is even more true of the Christian household as we seek to instill in our children the respect for authority taught by such passages as Titus 3:1 and Colossians 3:20. While it seems that fewer and fewer parents in our nation are concerned about developing this value in their children, it continues to be a strong parental message to the majority of children in our nation.

Unfortunately, parents rarely educate their children in the exceptions to this general rule of obedience. Consequently, our children are vulnerable to any adult who seeks to involve them in sexual activities by using the very training given by their parents. The simple fact of size difference between adult and child is enough to overcome much of a child's resistance to suggestions made by an adult, especially when that adult is a man. When this factor is combined with the child's blanket conditioning in obedience, that child becomes susceptible to sexual exploitation. Because of our failure to train our children in the one exception to the general rule of obedience, we have in effect conditioned them to be good candidates for sexual victimization.

In chapter 11, we will discuss at length different tools available to parents to help properly educate our children on whom to obey and when. It is important that we continue to teach them respect and obedience when relating to adults. However, it is equally important that we repeatedly make clear to them that there is one area in which they do not have to obey anyone. We must give them permission to say "no" when approached sexually.

Secrets That Enslave

Secrecy is an essential element in the continuation of any form of child sexual abuse. While teaching our children not to keep sexual secrets may not prevent an initial incident of abuse, it does make it impossible in most cases for the molester to continue the abuse. This applies equally to abuse within or outside of the family.

The first thing an abuser seeks to accomplish after the initial incident of sexual abuse is to insure that his actions will remain a secret. This is accomplished by any number of means, from engaging the child in a game of "this will be our special secret" to the extreme of murdering the victim. Even though the most gruesome and violent cases are usually the ones presented by the media, it should be understood that the use of violence in sexual abuse is the exception rather than the rule, whether the abuse occurs within or outside of the family.

In all but extreme cases, the reporting of the very first instance of sexual abuse, and therefore the prevention of any further abuse, can be accomplished by simply teaching children the difference between good secrets and bad secrets and giving them permission to tell their parents about the bad ones. By training them which secrets should not be kept and by reinforcing that concept regularly, we give our children permission to share their fears and hurts with us. Such permission will not only help protect our children but will enhance our communication with them. This concept of prevention will also be expanded upon later in chapter 11.

Parents may wonder why children would ever keep such a secret if indeed sexual abuse is as frightening and damaging as people say it is. There are probably as many answers to this question as there are children who have been molested. The pure intimidation of the molester's being an adult is important. Another important reason for such silence is the fact that the molester is often an adult loved and trusted by the child and the victim does not want to get that person or herself in trouble. Also, children often sense that if their parents learn what has happened to them, they would become emotionally upset or hurt. Or they fear, often with good reason, that if they report what happened to them, their parents will not believe them. One of the most common reasons children fail to report sexual abuse is that they usually believe they must have done something wrong to deserve what happened to them. Consequently, they hesitate to tell their parents for fear of the anger or punishment that may result.

These are only a few of the reasons that children do not report their own victimization. But whatever the reasons, the fact is that very few children ever report their abuse. They prefer to suffer in silence rather than face whatever real or imagined horrors await them if they tell. I have seen children who have been molested for years by someone outside of the home without the parents being in the least suspicious simply because the victims were afraid to tell anyone. Education and communication are important weapons for parents seeking to protect their children from this devastating problem.

The Incest Triangle

Throughout the literature available on the causes of child sexual abuse one encounters references to the "incest triangle." This is a term used to describe the dynamics within a typical incest family that allow sexual abuse to develop and continue. Just as the name implies, there are primarily three persons involved in the incest triangle: the non-offending caretaker (usually the mother), the molester, and the victim.

The mother in the incest family is usually an unwitting accomplice to the incest. She may be absent from the home much of the time due to illness or work scheduling. Or she may be unavailable altogether through death or divorce. Most incest treatment programs have found that a large majority of the mothers they deal with were themselves victims of sexual abuse as children. In such cases the mother's self-image has usually been damaged to the extent that she is subject to various emotional problems and sexual dysfunctions. These women tend to choose emotionally immature, domineering husbands who prefer social isolation and keep strict controls on all areas of family life. Also, because of their low self-image and dependency, these women tend to feel they cannot survive without their husbands.

Such a mother is usually not consciously aware of the relationship between her mate and her daughter. The daughter may have tried to tell her about the abuse indirectly through hints and clues. But these mothers often have so much to lose by recognizing sexual abuse that they choose to ignore the real message. The victim correctly perceives that telling her mother the whole story would cause great emotional damage, and so she chooses instead to suffer the abuse. Subconsciously, her mother may be relieved to be less and less the object of her husband's sexual demands and increasingly anxious to relinquish her role as mother within the family unit.

In regard to the molesters, we have learned through years of experience that these men are almost as likely to have been the victims of child sexual abuse as are their mates. They often appear from outside the family to be good fathers and husbands and are often hard-working, law-abiding individuals. However, they tend to be socially inadequate and unable to develop interpersonal relationships outside the family.

The molester is usually upset by what he perceives as his wife's sexual inadequacies and her failure to meet his emotional needs. However, he is seldom emotionally capable of talking to his wife about these problems and would never consider professional counseling. Instead of seeking emotional or sexual fulfillment outside the home where he feels uncomfortable, the molester often draws closer to his daughter, who also may feel emotionally rejected by her mother as time goes on. The daughter's normal desire for closeness and affection may be misinterpreted by the molester as a desire for sexual activity. Or he may simply decide to initiate sexual contact as the result of some twisted rationalization he has fabricated or conjured up in his own mind.

These fathers often seem unable to distinguish between love because of their backgrounds and emotional inadequacies. To the tional support involves sex. They may even convince themselves th daughters are actually in love with them or that they are saving their daughters from being initiated into the sexual world by some "young punk."

The victim finds herself in a trap. Her only options to continued abuse hold threats of destruction or at least tremendous damage to the family unit, particularly to her mother. Her father may promise her over and over while feeling the pangs of guilt that he will never molest her again, but she soon learns how empty those promises are. Her only choices are to tell or to suffer, and most victims choose to suffer.

In the next few chapters we will deal specifically with the damage that sexual abuse can cause in the lives of both incest victims and children molested outside of their families. It is my hope that, after reading this material, you will have a better understanding of why I have such respect and sympathy for the victims of sexual abuse, and why I want so desperately for Christians to lead the fight against this great evil.

A Driving Compulsion

We will thoroughly discuss the motivating factors, methods of operation, and rationalizations of sexual abusers later in this book. But I feel it is very important at this point for us to take a close look at one particular characteristic of molestation and its relationship to the abuser. That characteristic is the compulsive nature of child sexual abuse.

Parents, especially mothers of incest victims, have a tendency to believe the excuses and promises of a molester once abuse is uncovered. The tears, confessions, and even denials of these expert manipulators are usually very convincing. And, as we have just discussed, often the person learning of the abuse has her own reasons for not wanting to believe what has been reported. Because of these factors it is essential that what we are about to discuss be heard and understood by all parents.

Child sexual abuse, in its ongoing form, is a compulsive behavior. By this I mean that it is classified in the same general category as alcoholism and drug addiction in regard to the driving compulsion to continue the action. The dictionary defines a compulsion as "a strong, irresistible impulse." The more familiar we become with the subject of child sexual abuse, the more it seems to conform to that definition.

Sexual abuse often begins with an impulsive act which is more the result of circumstance than of planning. With that first act comes a mixture of pleasure and guilt. Unfortunately, pleasure has been shown in most instances to be stronger than guilt in determining human behavior. Consequently, even though a molester may feel tremendous guilt with each act of abuse, when another opportunity presents itself he will almost always continue to molest. The longer this behavior continues, the more difficult it is for the molester to stop himself from abusing.

An important aspect of compulsive behavior is that the more a person is under pressure, the more he is likely to give in to his compulsion. An alcoholic is more likely to drink when under pressure or depressed. The same holds true with child molestation, whether it be inside or outside of the family. A molester is more likely to repeat his crime when he is under pressure or feeling depressed, for whatever reason. This is why it is so ridiculous to assume that a molester will no longer sexually abuse children simply because he has been caught and will face stiff punishment if he should continue. In fact, he is actually more likely to repeat his offense at that point because of the fact that he is under pressure.

It is my special concern that any parent reading this chapter understand the compulsive nature of sexual abuse. If you as a parent have the slightest suspicion that your child has been the victim of sexual abuse, please take the time to read chapter 8 on the indicators of sexual abuse and to talk with your child. If your suspicions are confirmed, remember what we've discussed about the compulsive nature of sexual abuse and take whatever steps are necessary to protect your child. Above all, I beg you not to listen to the excuses and promises of the abuser, no matter how much you love that person. You are doing him no favor by letting the problem go unresolved.

Adding Fuel to the Flame

David Finkelhor, a famous researcher in the field of child sexual abuse, developed in 1981 a list of factors that might predispose adults toward the sexual abuse of children. He stated that there were four preconditions that had to be met before an adult could sexually abuse a child. First, the adult must have sexual feelings about children. Second, any internal inhibitors, such as conscience, must be overcome by the molester. Third, any external inhibitors, such as the presence of other adults, must be dealt with in order to provide the opportunity for the abuse and to prevent interference with it. And finally, the resistance of the child to the act of abuse must be overcome.[7]

Finkelhor learned that sexual feelings toward children can result from several different factors, including child pornography and advertising which sexualizes children. He also learned that alcohol was one effective means of overcoming internal inhibitors to sexual abuse. Other researchers have discussed at length the effects that certain drugs have in lowering moral inhibitions.

While the use of drugs and alcohol is by no means a prerequisite for sexual abuse, it does often contribute to the problem. A person normally having enough internal control to resist abusing a child may go over the line with even minimal amounts of alcohol or drugs. Again, this does not in any way excuse the molester from his actions. It is simply a statement of contributing factors.

Once conscience is removed as an obstacle to sexual victimization of children, it is little problem to create opportunities to molest a child and even less of a problem to overcome the resistance of the child. Children, in their innocence, have no defense against being hurt by those they love and trust. To protect these little ones from sexual victimization is up to us, the concerned adults in our society. By learning what causes this problem, we take the first step in its solution.

CHAPTER FOUR

A Child in Shock

We have been discussing thus far academic points on the existence of child sexual abuse and what factors are most evident as causes of this problem. For the next three chapters, we will be dealing with the most distressing subject in this book: the effects that child sexual abuse has on the victim and the victim's family. The fact that this subject requires three chapters to cover adequately is testimony to the serious nature of the problem.

In these chapters we will consider the effects of child sexual abuse in three separate segments. The first segment will deal with the initial effects on the victim resulting from the first incident of molestation. The second will have to do with the mid-range effects on the victim and the family if the molestation continues. In the third segment, we will look at the long-term effects of molestation on the victim and future generations of the victim's family.

It is important that we understand the extreme damage done to the victims of child sexual abuse for several reasons. First of all, it provides us with information necessary to refute the perverted claims of the "sex by eight or it's too late" groups such as the Rene Guyon Society and the North American Man/Boy Love Association (N.A.M.B.L.A.). While it is a moral indictment against our nation that we should even have to respond to such claims, the social and political reality is that these groups can and do have an influence on our system.

It is also important that we realize how sexual abuse damages its victims in order to develop some sympathy for these children rather than blaming them for their own abuse, which is the tendency of many. Additionally, being aware of the emotional impact of sexual abuse helps in developing treatments aimed specifically at these areas of damage. And, finally, knowing how sexual abuse is often passed from generation to generation will help us as parents and professionals to take the steps necessary to stop the sexual abuse cycle.

This first chapter on the effects of sexual abuse will give the reader a brief glance into the feelings experienced by a young victim during and after the first incident of abuse. If the victim's parent or parents have done their preventive homework, the abuse will be stopped with the first incident and emotional damage will be held to a minimum. If not, very probably the sexual exploitation of the victim will continue indefinitely.

Deeper Scars

A lot of attention has been focused in recent years on the subject of physical abuse of children—so much so that the term "child abuse" usually brings to mind images of bruised and battered children cowering under the raised fist of an angry parent. A great deal of this imagery is due to the simple fact that such things as bruises and cuts are visible signs of injury. We can see them and relate to the pain they must have caused. However, rarely do people stop to reflect on the fact that the real damage done in any form of child abuse is not physical but emotional. Only recently have we in America begun to realize that emotional damage done through child abuse appears to contribute heavily to such social ills as juvenile delinquency, violent crimes, drug and alcohol abuse, and self-destructive behavior.

Child sexual abuse seldom involves physical injury. There are some instances of sexual assault where force is used, and significant physical injury or even death may occur. However, this is the exception rather than the rule. Most sexual abuse begins with exposure or fondling and progresses gradually, often over a period of years, to more serious acts of abuse. The molester is often a parent or a loved and trusted relative or friend. In most instances these molesters take care not to damage the child physically. However, it is clear to many of us working in the treatment of these victims that simple physical injury, even if fairly severe, would have been preferable to the emotional damages we observe in these children. Physical injuries are usually quickly healed with the aid of physicians and modern medical technology. Emotional injuries are stubborn and elusive, taking much time and effort to heal and sometimes defying help altogether.

Professionals and parents must be made aware of the fact that the injuries suffered by the victims of sexual abuse are very real, even if they are not visible. We may be tempted to dismiss sexual abuse as not being harmful, especially when the child puts up a brave front in order to protect us from being hurt or when the abuser is someone both we and the child are close to. However, before we ignore the potential damage resulting from sexual abuse, let us first visit the confusing world of a child experiencing an act of sexual abuse.

Emotional Turmoil

Kathy is now six years old. She has a sister two years younger than she and a brother three years younger. Her father is a successful construction contractor and the family lives in a nice home. Her mother has been a caring parent who, until recently, showed her children a lot of affection. Kathy is not sure exactly when it started but for months now her mother has been gone a lot and has been spending less and less time with her children. She recently got a job working at a sporting goods store and sometimes works Saturdays and evenings.

Kathy's father and mother don't talk much or even see each other very much any more. However, Kathy hasn't seemed to notice this problem. She has been too busy enjoying the attention her father has been showing her lately. She has always loved her father and admired him very much. Recently, he has been talking to her a lot and even sharing his problems with her.

It is Friday night and Kathy's mother is working late doing inventory at the store. Her father sent her brother and sister to bed but let her stay up to watch television with him because she is older now and "getting to be a big girl." After watching television for a while on the couch, her father asks Kathy if she would like to sit on his lap. She eagerly accepts the offer and he holds her close. Kathy enjoys being close to her father. It is something that has seldom been available to her before. She snuggles even closer, happy to have this special attention.

It isn't long, however, before a different feeling begins to creep into Kathy's consciousness. She doesn't know what the feeling is or where it comes from. She only knows that it makes her uncomfortable. Her stomach feels funny and the warmness seems to be going away. Kathy realizes now that her father has begun to rub her back and legs very softly and slowly. Even though this feels good, there is something strange about what is happening. She snuggles closer hoping the bad feelings will go away, but they only seem to get worse.

Her father begins haltingly to rub her chest and stomach. Kathy can sense that her father is changing. She does not know how or why but she knows he is changing. The feeling in her stomach steadily grows to a panic. As her father softly tells her what a pretty girl she is, he begins to fondle her. He is trembling. Kathy is paralyzed with fear. She wants to ask her father what he is doing, but a voice inside warns her not to speak or to cry out. She can do nothing but remain motionless, tense, as her father continues to caress her.

Finally, Kathy's panic overcomes her inner voice and she shakily asks her father why he is doing that. As he withdraws his hand abruptly, he mumbles something about just wanting to touch her because he loves her. Kathy looks up to see fear on her father's face. He explains to her that he was just trying to show her a special kind of love and that they should keep that special kind of love a secret between the two of them because nobody else would understand. It is especially important that Kathy not tell her mother as she might become upset or even angry with Kathy. The urgency in her father's voice tells Kathy that it is a very important secret and a lot is at stake if this secret gets out.

Nothing more happens as they continue to watch television, but the closeness Kathy had felt does not return. As she lies in bed trying to go to sleep, Kathy is totally confused. She cries but does not know why. She feels as if she did something wrong but does not know what it could have been. She thinks of asking her mother about it but then she remembers her father's warning. She also remembers that her mother had been easily upset recently and she probably would be mad like her father said. Not knowing what to do or where to turn, Kathy can do nothing but cry and stare at the wall of her room. Finally she falls asleep from sheer exhaustion.

Kathy's story is a common one. It is repeated untold thousands of times each year in the United States. In her particular case, the initial incident of molestation was incestuous and involved her natural father. However, the feelings she was experiencing are also reported by children who have suffered molestation at the hands of other trusted adult authority figures. In fact, many of those same feelings are evident in cases of sibling incest and even sexual abuse by strangers. As we work with various children who have been victimized and talk to other professionals doing the same, it becomes clear that there are a number of emotions which come into play in cases of initial molestation. Those encountered most often are fear and confusion, along with feelings of betrayal, guilt, and helplessness.

Fear is a completely understandable emotion in such situations. Since most sexual abuse begins when a child is quite young, the victim has little or no experience or knowledge with which to interpret what is happening to her. Also, as the molester becomes increasingly sexually excited during the episode, some inexplicable changes take place in his behavior and even his body. To see someone she is close to and familiar with change in such strange ways so quickly is a frightening experience for a child. The look on his face, the rate of his breathing, and his trembling excitement are all new and disturbing to her. She may see a normally controlled and loving person change to an obsessed and seemingly uncontrollable animal in a matter of minutes. Suddenly she is in the presence of someone she does not know and is afraid of what this new person may do to her.

It is hard even to imagine the fear in the hearts of these children as they face this ordeal. But don't doubt for a minute that the fear is there. I have seen it many times in the eyes of children as they relate having been sexually abused. Even if the abuse lasts for many years, somehow they always seem to vividly remember that first incident, and with the memories come the tears.

Confusion is another emotion common to the victim of child sexual abuse, especially in the case of incest. Before the abuse began, Kathy was as a child should be, trusting, dependent, carefree, and innocent. With one act of abuse she became the keeper of a dreadful family secret. She is made to feel responsible for her mother's continued happiness and perhaps even the very existence of the family as she knows it. If such terrible burdens result from a comparatively mild instance of abuse, you can well imagine how children feel who are threatened with violence or told by their molesters that "your mother would die if she ever found out." These children face total confusion about their role in the family and how this act is going to change their lives and the lives of those they love.

Another emotion expressed by many of these children when they report their first incident of sexual abuse is a feeling of betrayal. This is especially true of older victims who are more aware of what has happened to them. While this feeling is understandably absent in many cases of abuse outside the family, the position of trust held by the adult in an incestuous relationship causes the victim to feel betrayed by the molester. Even younger children may not understand the act itself but can tell by the way the perpetrator acted that it was wrong. Otherwise, why would it be such an important secret to keep? It is a terrible thing to realize that a person you love and trust and upon whom you depend for your care and protection has betrayed that trust.

On top of all this comes a feeling of guilt which may affect the child victim for years to come. Children in our society are conditioned to believe that if they are hurt, it must somehow have been their fault. If a child comes running to a parent with an injury, the parent often responds with a statement like, "Well, what did you do this time?" A sexually abused child almost always accepts the guilt for her abuse, even if she does not fully understand what happened. She knows she was hurt, confused, or scared, so she must have been somewhere she should not have been or done something she should not have done. I know of children who were dragged off a playground and molested yet were convinced that they were somehow at fault for what had happened to them. It is little wonder that in the treatment of these children we spend much of our time saying, "it is not your fault—you are not to blame for what happened to you." It is amazing to me that we should even have to mention such a thing to a victim, let alone work so hard to convince her she is innocent of any blame.

The emotions and feelings we have been discussing in this chapter often converge on the child victim of sexual abuse, even if the abuse is a one-time occurrence. Some victims are more fortunate and, depending on the circumstances of the abuse, are not as dramatically affected. However, for the less fortunate, there develops a feeling of total helplessness. To tell would be to risk the wrath of the molester and possibly to destroy the family. To remain in silence is to risk further abuse. Such heavy burdens for such small shoulders! With one self-centered act by a thoughtless adult comes the death of a child's innocence, a death for which there can be no resurrection.

CHAPTER FIVE

Within a
Nightmare

Having just discussed the emotional effects of short-term sexual abuse, we need now to consider an area even more distasteful. Once a child has been sexually abused and the abuse has been discovered, drastic measures must be taken to prevent further abuse. Otherwise, it is usually a certainty that this same child will continue to be molested, often for a period of years. While this is obviously not the case with a one-time act by a stranger, if the molester is a trusted adult having even occasional access to the victim, the molestation usually continues—even after discovery—if proper precautions are not taken.

More specific information on why discovery and threats are not effective in stopping sexual abuse will be covered later in this book and should be carefully considered, especially by the parent of the victim. However, in this chapter we will be considering the effects of sexual abuse on victims and their families when the abuse is for some reason allowed to continue, with or without the knowledge of the victim's parent or parents.

Trust and Intimacy as Casualties

When molestation continues to occur past the initial incident, the offender is usually an adult trusted by the victim. The adult in question will often tell the child after each incident of molestation that he is sorry and promises that it will never happen again. After dealing with many families regarding this problem I have come to believe that the molester often means what he says when he makes such a promise and realizes what he has done is very wrong. However, almost invariably he repeats his offense at the next opportunity. Time after time I have heard victims sob, "He said he was sorry and that he would never do it again, but he lied."

Brandy was six years old when she was first molested by her father. After several incidents of fondling and exposure, Brandy became so frightened that she talked to her grandmother about what was happening. Fortunately she was believed and her father was confronted with the abuse. He admitted to his problem and the family decided to handle it themselves by having Brandy live with her grandparents. After two years of separation Brandy's father argued convincingly that it was now safe for her to return home as he was "better" and had a new wife who could fully meet his sexual needs. He promised the grandparents and Brandy that there would be no further abuse. Within a week of her return home Brandy had been molested again by her father. Her feelings of betrayal and confusion were so strong that Brandy could not tell anyone. She gave up on being rescued. It wasn't until Brandy was nine that our department first learned of this case. A local hospital reported suspicion of abuse based on severe vaginal injuries. When Brandy was interviewed at the hospital it was learned that she was injured during an incident of rape by her father. Brandy had resisted the assault and had been held down by her stepmother.

Tragically, in cases such as Brandy's the mistrust and suspicion the victim has come to feel toward the offender is almost always applied to adults in general and will often adversely affect her relationships with the adult world for much of her life. Women who have been sexually abused as children usually find it hard to trust any adult male.

Once a child's trust has been repeatedly betrayed by someone who is supposed to protect and care for her, an emotional and sometimes physical tension sets in which makes it difficult for the child to relax. Since she has learned she cannot fully trust adults, it becomes necessary for her to protect herself. I remember several different little girls who related going to bed fully clothed or wearing multiple layers of clothing in order to make being molested more difficult. The pathetic mechanisms these children contrive to avoid further abuse are heartbreaking. To see a child constantly tense and suspicious of any move toward her or even the most innocent touch by an adult is to see emotional harm at its ugliest.

Tina is now sixteen. She has been molested by her grandfather, who lives with the family, since she was eleven years old. A school friend she had confided in reported the abuse to a counselor. Unfortunately, living five years in the constant fear of molestation had already taken a terrible emotional toll on

Tina. Recently her mother was contacted by the high school after a male teacher had put his hand on Tina's shoulder to get her attention and she had exploded into hysterical screaming. Unfortunately, this has not been an isolated occurrence. Tina is sent to the office two or three times a month for similar hysterical episodes.

Often, such extreme stress and tension take a physical toll on the victim. It is not uncommon to see children who are so afraid to sleep for fear of being abused that they stay awake all night and sleep whenever they can during the day, often at school. They appear exhausted or depressed and are unable to explain the reason for their behavior to their teachers or other concerned adults. The sad part is that even such vigilance and tension provide little or no deterrent to the molester.

Just as with trust, intimacy is an early casualty of continuing sexual abuse. The victim learns quickly that it is not safe to innocently ask for affection, closeness, or emotional support. A simple show of affection can result in a confusing and painful experience. Not surprisingly, the child victim develops the attitude that it is not worth the risk to be honest or close. Again, these feelings overlap into a child's relationship with adults other than the molester and even into peer relationships. Eventually, as we shall later see, they set the stage for ruined marriages and the continuation of the abuse cycle.

The Loss of Childhood

As sexual abuse continues within a home, a massive confusion develops within the child's mind. At one moment, she is an object of sexual desire, to be wooed and courted. She even has some degree of control over the adult while advances are being made. Then, immediately following the abuse, she again becomes a dominated child—without control—subject to the orders and discipline of adults. This lover-child confusion is an almost universal outgrowth of incestuous relationships. The victim is robbed of her right to a clearly defined role within the family and instead is forced to float between the adult world and the world of children.

Often going hand in hand with the lover-child confusion is what I refer to as the "little mother syndrome." The fact that most non-offending caretakers (usually mothers) were sexually molested themselves as children contributes heavily to this phenomenon. Because of her own molestation as a child, the mother often suffers from difficulties in regard to intimacy and sexual adjustment. Rather than fight the developments in the family, of which she is often vaguely aware, she may choose to remove herself gradually from the role of mother. As this transition takes place, the child often takes on an increasing number of motherly duties, including care of the younger children, a larger share of the household chores, and the position of emotional confidante to the father. Assuming the role of his sexual partner seems almost to be a logical step in this progression of errors.

My first sexual abuse case as a social worker was an excellent example of this dynamic. Warned by a local teacher that one of her eighth grade girls was showing behavior indicative of sexual abuse, I responded to the school and interviewed the girl. She related that both she and her older sister had been sexually molested by their natural father for a number of years. Following my interview with this girl I talked to her older sister at their home. She too related a story of sexual abuse which began when she was six. As a result of their statements, both girls were taken into protective custody. Also in the home was a younger brother, and it was necessary to transport him to the home of a relative before taking the oldest girl to a foster home. During the entire trip to the relative's home, this poor girl was instructing her brother on what to tell their mother, when to feed the dog, how to do his chores, what clothes to wear to school the next day, and many other motherly details I could not possibly recall. All this took place while she was sobbing uncontrollably. There was little doubt who the mother was in their family.

The little mother syndrome is an important indicator of sexual abuse and is seen with shocking regularity in sexually abusive families. Yet such behavior is too often overlooked or dismissed as being indicative of a "very responsible young lady who cares about her sisters and brothers." That is not to say that a child helping with the household chores and participating in child care should lead one to suspect sexual abuse. But when a child, for all intents and purposes, takes on the role of mother and wife within a family, a closer examination of the situation is warranted.

The emotional damage done to the victim in such a role reversal is largely due to the fact that she is not allowed to have her own dependency needs met during her childhood. She is expected to parent her parents as well as her brothers and sisters. No one asks her what her needs are, nor do they allow her the luxury of a carefree childhood. This not only causes damage to the child but often contributes to the perpetuation of the sexual abuse cycle, as we shall see later in this book.

Another aspect of sexual abuse which tends to rob the victim of her childhood is the unconscious training she receives in seductive behavior. Once sexual abuse begins, the relationship between the victim and the offender becomes predominantly sexual in nature. The child learns that to please the adult and protect herself, sexual favors must be granted. Since physical force or threats are seldom used in incestuous relationships, the child is not giving in from fear of harm but rather from a desire to please or the simple intimidation of being a powerless child in a world of powerful adults.

The outgrowth of early conditioning in victims is often a tendency to relate to others in a sexual or seductive manner. These children have been taught to obtain the attention they require through sexualized behavior. Even though victims have no choice but to learn this method of interaction with others, they are often later condemned as seductive or "over-sexed" and are even blamed for their own molestation. "Obviously," it is said, "she seduced him." I have too often heard this ridiculous accusation made, even in regard to children as young as three years of age!

> Christie is now twelve. She has been molested by her father since the age of eight. An only child, Christie was regularly reminded by her father that he had wanted a boy. He showed her almost no attention until becoming interested in her sexually. Even though Christie was afraid and confused by the sexual activity, it was the only time her father paid her any attention at all. She quickly learned that sexualized behavior was an effective means of gaining the approval and the attention of men. Since Christie had never been taught to seek attention in more appropriate ways, it was to be expected that she would relate seductively to all males. It was because of this conditioning that Christie had also been molested by an uncle, her grandfather, and a soccer coach at school. When these incidents came to light, attorneys for the molesters successfully argued that Christie was at fault for seducing these men.

It is obvious from the abundance of stories such as Christie's that society, to this point, has been unable to accept the simple truth that a child's seductive behavior is the *result* rather than the cause of her molestation. A child who has been not only sexually abused but condemned as the cause of her own molestation has been victimized twice—once by the molester and again by society.

It is little wonder that a child, being faced with such a terrible problem and having nowhere to turn for help, will often regress emotionally in an effort to deal with the pressures so cruelly forced upon her. It is not at all uncommon to see a victim of sexual abuse regress to a happier time when all she had to be concerned with were dolls, toys, and an occasional skinned knee. To be responsible for an entire family at such an early age is a tremendous burden and escaping emotionally is one alternative to living in such a demanding role.

The Fragmented Family

As children continue to be molested within a family unit, the dynamics of sexual abuse eat away at the family structure. This process is slow and devastating, as are many of Satan's most effective tools. Gradual changes are more likely to go unnoticed and are therefore less likely to be dealt with. The deterioration of relationships within the family can be compared to the growth process in our children. We as parents do not notice their growth because we see them every day. However, a relative or friend might be shocked at how much the children have grown since their last visit. The same principle can be applied to sexual abuse. The damage is gradual and even those directly affected are not aware of its extent.

Usually, the first family relationship to be affected by sexual abuse after that of the victim and offender is the relationship between the parents or caretakers. These marriages often appear to be stable from the outside because of their commonly long duration and a seeming lack of marital discord. Within the family itself, however, it is quite a different story. We have found in dealing with these families that most of the non-molesting partners, usually the mothers, were themselves molested as children. Because of this they find themselves more easily emotionally detached from their husbands. After all, they were taught by their own experiences that men are not to be trusted and are "only after one thing."

On the other hand, her husband finds emotional solace in a young child who is non-threatening, trusting, and always available. Thus it is not long before the emotional detachment between the caretakers is complete and they live in separate emotional worlds with no intimate communication. After the discovery of abuse it becomes a major task to build communication between the parents. Needless to say, the whole problem could have been avoided had the parents developed communication and intimacy in their own relationship from the start, but it is the victim who has had to pay the price for their failure to do so. In considering these and other factors in sexual abuse, it should be constantly kept in mind that the molester and the molester *alone* is responsible for his actions. No amount of emotional or sexual deprivation, frustration, or social circumstances justify the sexual molestation of a child.

Another family casualty to be considered in the development of sexual abuse is the relationship between the victim and the non-offending parent. As the offender pays more and more attention to the victim and often openly courts her, the mother becomes jealous. It is common for the offender to confide things to his daughter that he would not to his wife. The victim, seeking to please her father, will listen and often be sympathetic. Consequently, the offender prefers his daughter's company to that of his wife, causing further jealousy and emotional detachment.

As the relationship continues and the child becomes increasingly uncomfortable with its sexual nature, she will often attempt to disclose the abuse in the hope that her mother will intervene. However, she is torn between her desire for help and the fear that her mother will be hurt by the situation. Consequently, her cries for help often take the form of hints and strategically placed clues. Victims often use statements such as "I hate staying home with Daddy" to alert their mothers. Or they will leave blood-stained sheets or underpants where their mother will see them. It is an unusual child who has the strength to tell her mother directly what is happening.

Unfortunately, the victim's mother is often unable to get the message. It is not easy to recognize a fact which would likely destroy a long-standing marriage, leave her without a means of support, make her the sole caretaker of her children, and send her husband to jail. I remember a particular case in which a victim had sent her brother to tell her mother that "Dad is messing around with my sister." Although the mother acknowledged that her son had indeed delivered such a message, she claimed that she had no idea what had been meant by "messing around." That mother had a tremendous investment in not hearing what her daughter was trying to tell her. Because of such failures on the part of the non-offending caretakers to listen and intervene, it is common for victims to develop a deep-seated resentment toward their mothers.

The third area of fragmentation within the family occurs in relation to the victim's siblings. The fact that the offender spends a great deal of his time and attention on one child leads to jealousy on the part of her brothers and sisters. She often receives special favors and seems to be the one who always gets to go places with her father. At the same time, because of her new role as mother, she is required to be an authority figure to her siblings, which only adds to the resentment.

Later, when the victim can no longer bear to put up with the abuse, she is usually blamed and angrily denounced by her siblings for reporting the abuse and breaking up the family. That condemnation, coupled with the fact that the victim's mother often believes the offender rather than her daughter, compounds the victim's self-condemnation and isolation. Child molestation, therefore, commonly leaves in its path a family splintered on many levels. Without a great deal of prayer and extensive counseling, such a family has little chance of survival.

Poor Peer Relationships

Not only does the child victim find herself isolated from her family members. She also usually experiences isolation from her peers as the result of the dynamics of sexual abuse. As previously discussed, the victim has been taught to relate sexually and has not been able to develop other social skills. If she attempts to relate sexually to her peers, especially during her younger years, she soon learns that such behavior is unacceptable. Lacking any other means of social interaction, it is not uncommon for the victim to withdraw. What social contact she does have may occur during a period of regression which places her below the age level of other children. Or, it may be that she attempts to relate to other children on a pseudo-mature level which often results from the little mother syndrome. This places her above the age level of her peers. Both approaches cause alienation from her peer group. She is condemned as being a baby or is shunned for being bossy.

Peer relationships are further complicated by another phenomenon often observed in sexual abuse victims. As the abuse continues and the child is powerless to prevent it, resentment and anger build to the point where they must be expressed. These feelings often take the form of violent behavior toward younger or weaker children. The victim realizes it is not safe to express her anger toward the offender and consequently that anger is displaced on a less threatening object. Such behavior only adds to the victim's isolation.

A factor which often influences the victim to impose upon herself a degree of voluntary isolation is her fear that her molestation is somehow visible to others. As we have seen previously, a molested child usually accepts the blame, feeling she must have done something to deserve what happened to her. As a result, she feels dirty, scarred, and inwardly ugly. Through some psychological process not fully understood, victims often come to believe that others can tell they have been molested simply by looking at them, especially if they are not clothed. Obviously, such a belief has no basis in fact. Nevertheless, it is a very real concern to the victim and has been instrumental in the discovery of many cases of sexual abuse. Such children may refuse to suit up for P.E. or take showers for fear that the abuse is somehow visible on their bodies. Some victims actually believe their abuse is visible even when they are fully clothed. It is easy to see how such a belief could have a decidedly negative effect on their peer relationships.

The final and most decisive factor in the isolation of the victim from her peers and from society at large is the fear and jealousy of the molester. With the very first act of sexual abuse, the offender is vulnerable to discovery. He is well aware of society's taboo against such actions and is also vaguely aware of the possible legal consequences. As the molestation continues, it becomes more and more likely that his actions will be observed or that his victim will say something to someone about what is happening. As stated in John 3:20, a person doing evil hates the light. Secrecy is essential in evil activities and sexual abuse is no exception. Whether the abuse occurs within or outside the family, the message to the victim is the same. "This must be our secret."

There are two basic options available to the molester in his effort to keep his acts secret. Either option may be employed separately by the offender, or they may be used in combination. The first is the use of threats. Sometimes threats of physical violence are made, but more commonly the threats play on the child's love for her family. Several I seem to hear regularly are "if you tell, your mother will be mad at both of us"; "if you tell, I will go to jail"; "if you tell, the family will break up and they will put you in a foster home"; and "if you won't help me, maybe your sister will."

All of these threats put the responsibility for the family's welfare and even its very existence squarely on the shoulders of the victim and compound the emotional damage already being done. Repeated often enough, they are usually accepted as truth by the child. Indeed, their effectiveness in preventing disclosure appears to be due in large measure to the element of truth they contain. The child is aware that her mother would not be emotionally able to cope with such a report. Likewise, she may already have noticed the offender paying more attention to her sister. What she is usually not aware of is that quite possibly he is already molesting her sister and using the same "line" to assure her sister's cooperation. Such arrangements are quite common in incestuous families with more than one girl.

The second option for assuring secrecy basically consists of seeking to convince the child that the molestation is nothing out of the ordinary and is even educational or beneficial. However, the offender is careful to stress that this is to be a special secret between the two of them. Since secrecy in such cases is possible only as long as the child is ignorant of the true nature of the act, the molester must somehow insure that the victim is not educated in the truth. Consequently, he refuses to allow the child to receive any form of sex education, even if such education is presented from a Christian perspective.

This is not to imply that Christian parents who object to sexual education are molesting their children. On the contrary—it is the responsibility of Christian parents to monitor such educational material and refuse it when inappropriate. However, it is also their responsibility to assure that their children are provided with an appropriate and complete education in this very important area. Later in this book we will consider different materials and programs appropriate for such purposes.

Education is only one area the offender must be concerned with in protecting himself. He must also prevent his victim from obtaining information from her peers. Consequently, an abusing father or stepfather will often refuse to allow the victim to attend school functions, social activities, or outings where she will be in contact with other children or trusted adults. The more contact she has with others her age, the more likely it is that she will learn the socially unacceptable nature of what is being done to her.

When the victim reaches dating age, the molester's efforts at isolating her are often complicated by jealousy. The thought of sharing the attentions of the victim with possible boyfriends can drive a molester to extreme acts of jealousy. Frantic attempts are made to insure that competitors for the victim's attention are discouraged.

Nancy has been molested by her father since she was in second grade. He had succeeded in keeping her more or less isolated from others her age during her grade school years. However, she has now been in high school for two years and has been demanding more and more that she be able to date and spend time with her friends. Her father has made every effort to discourage boys showing an interest in her. He subjects them to confrontive interviews on their "intentions" and sets down many rules for dating. Before and after each date he insists on kissing Nancy on the mouth and as often as not will require sexual intercourse as a condition of her being able to go on a date. He also sits up anxiously waiting for her return and questions her about what happens on each date. Nancy has seriously considered joining a friend who plans to run away and live in Los Angeles.

Ironically, it is usually such displays of "juvenile" jealousy that provide the needed incentive for the victim to escape the abusive family. Where love and concern for the protection of the family had previously prevented her from reporting, the victim is now forced to take action by the molester's extreme behavior. Unfortunately, by that time the damage has already been done.

Damaged Goods—The Corrosion of Self-Image

In the previous chapter we dealt to a limited extent with the guilt experienced by the victim of sexual abuse. Children are programmed to believe that if they have been hurt, it must be because of something they did wrong. As sexual abuse continues, that belief is reinforced. The fact that the victim occasionally experiences physical pleasure during the sexual activity serves to intensify her guilt. She does not realize that the pleasure she experiences is an involuntary physiological response to sexual stimulation and does not in any way indicate her consent to the molestation itself.

The increasing feelings of guilt on the part of the victim have a disastrous effect on her already fragile self-image. Barraged with threats and negative statements and deprived of positive input from others, she comes to believe that she deserves her victimization. This conviction becomes a self-fulfilling prophecy as her behavior begins to reflect her self-hatred. She accepts the role of a victim, considering herself to be "damaged goods," robbed of her innocence, good for nothing but to be abused and misused.

The outgrowth of the damaged goods syndrome in a sexual abuse victim can take many forms. Some of the more common behavioral outgrowths among victims are sexual promiscuity, prostitution, self-abusive behavior, criminal activity, and violence. Promiscuity is very common, especially among teenage victims, and often is used against them as proof that they are of loose moral character and are therefore either lying about the abuse or caused the problem by seducing the adult.

After interviewing many adults who had been molested as children, it became clear to me that most of these victims had experienced periods of extreme sexual promiscuity during or after their victimization. Those periods of exaggerated and indiscriminate sexual activity lasted anywhere from a few months to a decade. The victims usually spoke of having had overwhelming feelings of worthlessness and victimization during those times. Many women described that period in their lives as being a desperate search for love, acceptance, and affection. Unfortunately, they had been taught to relate only on a sexual level and relationships begun on that level were seldom positive, meaningful, or longlasting.

Mickie is now thirty-four years old. She has been married twice and has two children. Currently divorced, she has no plans of ever beginning another relationship with a man. In fact, she finds it difficult at this point even to be in the same room with men. Mickie was molested from age nine to age fifteen by her father, who was a minister. She was made to feel as if it were her fault because she was so "pretty" and her father said he found her to be "irresistible." By the time she left home, Mickie had come to consider herself as worthless and having nothing to offer but her body. For two years after leaving home she was extremely promiscuous, seeking acceptance and attention in the only way she knew. Unfortunately, the men she met seemed always to turn out to be abusive and exploitive. Mickie has never had a positive relationship with a man. She becomes physically ill when in close proximity to men. The only supportive figures in her life have been female. Even though she finds the idea morally repulsive, Mickie feels herself being attracted to women she knows to be lesbians.

Prostitution is another commonly observed outgrowth of sexual abuse and seems almost to be a logical step in the progression of emotional damage done to the victim. Through his actions the molester has, without realizing it, trained the victim toward that end. While in her home, the victim has been required to pay sexually for affection and attention which should have been provided to her freely as a dependent child. Instead of protecting her, the molester in a very real sense requires his victim to prostitute herself in order to meet her own needs and insure the emotional survival of her mother and the continuation of the family unit. Thus, it should come as no shock when a girl, running from sexual abuse within her family, ends up as a prostitute in one of our cities.

In a recent survey of adolescent prostitutes in Minneapolis, 75 percent reported being victims of incestuous relationships. While there is no proof that the incest itself caused those girls to turn to prostitution, there would appear to be an obvious connection between the two. Even early research on this subject indicated a link between sexual abuse and prostitution. For example, in a study done in 1942, Paul Sloone and Eva Karpinsky found that in one of every three cases in their study of father-daughter incest, the victim reported having gone through a period of prostitution.[8] Again, such behavior becomes understandable when we consider that the victim already feels used and good for nothing but to be taken advantage of.

While promiscuity and prostitution are in a very real sense self-abusive behavior, the outworking of a low self-image is often expressed more directly. Self-mutilation is not all that uncommon among sexual abuse victims. One girl in my caseload actually cut her face with razor blades to demonstrate what she thought of herself. However, most victims do not resort to such direct methods of self-punishment but will instead unconsciously recruit others to reinforce their feelings of worthlessness. One of the most common examples of such behavior is the victim who, without realizing what she is doing, will seek out and marry an abusive partner. In this way she receives the punishment she feels she deserves without having to administer it herself. This dynamic will be dealt with more precisely in chapter 6.

The Root of Bitterness

Another tool Satan effectively uses in his attempt to destroy the family through sexual abuse is bitterness. At the same time the victim's self-image is being systematically destroyed, she experiences a growing resentment toward the abuser and toward the non-abusing parent. At first she is confused about what is happening and may enjoy the attention and closeness. However, the message becomes increasingly clear that this activity is to be kept a secret at all costs. She also can tell from the molester's actions and attitude that this is not just any secret. It is very important, and a lot depends on its being kept secret.

The abuse itself usually progresses gradually from fondling and "lesser" forms of molestation to sexual intercourse. I say "lesser" because many people consider these forms of sexual abuse to be less harmful. In actuality, I have found very little difference in the emotional harm caused by fondling and that caused by intercourse. The real issue is the betrayal of trust.

The age at which actual intercourse occurs, if it does occur, may vary considerably. I have had several cases where intercourse began at six or seven years of age and have heard of many cases of even earlier onset. However, a more representative age bracket would be eleven to thirteen years of age. In one case I dealt with, the victim convinced her father that she should be a virgin when she married. Consequently, he agreed to stop short of intercourse during the first twenty years of abuse. However, when she did marry he then demanded intercourse since virginity was no longer an issue. The molestation continued for several years after her marriage.

In long-term sexual abuse, the victim feels more emotionally uncomfortable as the molestation continues. The innocent pleasure of closeness and attention soon are gone and a loathing of the acts themselves, and the molester in particular, grows steadily. Her increasing anger at being robbed of her childhood and betrayed can be difficult to control. When combined with the jealousy and possessiveness commonly displayed by the molester during the dating years, that anger often leads to confrontations which result in the victim leaving home. If she leaves without reporting, the offender will often then concentrate his efforts on a younger sister, whom he has probably already begun to molest. It is a constant source of amazement to those of us working in this field that there always seems to be a younger sister available.

As the victim of sexual abuse leaves her home, she takes with her a deep-seated anger and bitterness toward her abuser. The hatred she feels, even if more for the act than for the abuser, seems never to leave her at peace. In time she may come to understand that the offender's actions resulted from his "sickness." But her bitterness will taint any positive memories she has of the molester until it is effectively dealt with through prayer and Bible-centered counseling.

Another bitterness almost universally developed by the victim in a sexually abusive family is that directed toward the mother or non-offending caretaker. Children, especially younger children, feel that somehow, perhaps by some sort of magic, adults are aware of everything that happens in their lives. Parents seem to be able to tell just by looking at them whether they are happy or sad and even whether they are lying or telling the truth. This childish belief in the all-knowing parent seems to carry over into the dynamics of sexual abuse. The victim feels that her mother did know or at least should have known about the molestation. Perhaps she even gave her mother a few hints. Then why didn't her mother stop the abuse? Why did her mother allow her to suffer all that time without helping?

These feelings on the part of the victim are reinforced by comments the molester makes over a long period of time. He may say, "Your mother doesn't want me to hug and kiss her and I need you to help me," or, "Your mother is sick and can't do what mommies are supposed to do with daddies." He implies that it is her mother's fault that his "needs" are not being met and it is the child's responsibility to help meet those needs. Her mother may inadvertently lend credibility to these manipulative claims by becoming emotionally detached from the family and seeming to ignore any signs of the problem.

It is easy to see how the victim often has more bitterness toward the non-offending parent than she does toward the molester, even if her mother had no conscious knowledge of the molestation. After all, the offender has had years to convince the victim that the fault is not his. Rebuilding the relationship between mother and daughter in such cases is a long and laborious process. However, it is the key element in the survival of the family unit and as such is a primary target in treatment.

Another important consideration in regard to bitterness and anger is the result they have on the victim's social adjustment. For various reasons, victims of sexual abuse, no matter what their age, are seldom able to strike out at the true objects of their hatred. Consequently, they have the choice of sublimating their feelings or hurting others more defenseless than themselves. Most victims of sexual abuse choose to sublimate or live with their bitterness, hurting no one but themselves. There are some, however, who choose to take out their anger on whatever or whoever is available and vulnerable. Recent studies of prison populations indicate that histories of child sexual abuse are much more common among inmates than among control groups within the community at large. This seems especially to be true in regard to sex offenses and violent crimes.

A case recently in the news presents a good example of the extreme effects that sexual abuse can have on a victim. A fourteen-year-old girl was convicted of first degree murder in the brutal stabbing of an eighty-five-year-old woman. The girl reportedly recorded the incident in her diary by writing, "Today Cindy and I ran away and killed an old lady. It was lots of fun." This same fourteen-year-old girl had reported to the police some months earlier that she had been molested by her father since she was three years of age. Her father had spent time in jail for the reported offense. It is not my purpose to suggest that being sexually abused as a child is an excuse for illegal or anti-social behavior. However, recognizing that child sexual abuse can and does have a causative effect in such cases should help convince us of the seriousness of the problem and the importance of treatment and prevention.

Attempted Escape

We have been discussing in this chapter the extensive damage caused by long-term sexual abuse of children. Keeping in mind the pain, confusion, and emotional trauma just described, it becomes easier for us to understand the behavior of many victims as they seek desperately to escape further abuse. Nearly all victims attempt, in one form or another, to escape at some point during their victimization. Some have the strength to try one means after another until they eventually succeed. Other less fortunate children make one or two attempts at escape and, when they fail, seem never to have the strength to try again. Unfortunately, we encounter too many children who fall into the second category.

Escape attempts may take a number of different forms. Perhaps the most common form is emotional escape. Many times the victim, with good reason, feels she is unable to actually remove herself from the home because of her age, fear, or lack of resources. However, her severe emotional distress requires that she find a way to escape the abuse. Consequently, it is not unusual to find a victim who has learned to mentally remove herself from the sexual acts themselves even as they occur. One girl we worked with in counseling said she would conjugate French verbs while the abuse was occurring. Another imagined that she became a piece of furniture in the room, and another "melted into the wall." Many victims report that during each incident of abuse they felt as if their minds had left their bodies and they had somehow become impartial observers of the act itself. It was as if they were watching someone else being molested.

This mechanism is often observed in victims of sexual abuse and is quite understandable. Unable to escape physically and emotionally incapable of reporting the abuse, the victim is forced to submit to the act itself. However, facing such total betrayal by someone she loves is so emotionally threatening that the victim must mentally remove herself from the sexual act in order to maintain her sanity. The resulting mental gymnastics are a pitiful attempt on the part of the child to deal with this severe emotional conflict. For some, such efforts provide a limited and temporary escape. Others are left to deal with the devastation in any way they can, some even retreating to the total fantasy world of psychosis.

Another means of escape often used by the victim of sexual abuse is alienation of the molester. The victim, consciously or unconsciously, sets about to make herself physically unattractive or behaviorally repulsive to the molester. Attempts at alienation may take several different forms. Some of the more common are overeating, poor personal hygiene, and hostile, acting-out behavior.

> Jennifer is twelve. Her stepfather has been molesting her since she was nine. She is afraid to tell her mother, who already has emotional problems. Also, her stepfather has warned her that if she tells she will be placed in a foster home. Jennifer knows that her stepfather does not like "fat" women because he is always after her mother to lose weight. About a year ago Jennifer began to eat compulsively. When her stepfather complained about her weight, she ate even more. Unfortunately, Jennifer's weight gain had little effect as far as reducing her stepfather's sexual demands. Even though being overweight did not protect Jennifer from being molested, she continued to eat excessively. Eating seemed to relieve some of her tension and made her feel a little better, at least for a while.

It is quite common in talking with previous victims of sexual abuse to hear accounts of girls who would purposely overeat in an attempt to make themselves "fat and ugly." It was hoped that their obesity would cause the molester to lose interest in them sexually. Similarly, other victims described their total neglect of personal hygiene in order to make themselves repulsive. Both of these behaviors are not only common but almost to be expected as logical outgrowths and expressions of the victim's poor self-image and feelings of worthlessness. Unfortunately, neither seems to be effective in preventing continued abuse, and both tend to be carried over into the victim's adult life, often adversely affecting their social adjustment.

Hostile behavior toward the molester is also a commonly observed tool used by the victim in her attempt to escape, but is generally seen in older victims. Because of the dynamics of power and intimidation, very few young victims choose to risk the wrath of the molester through such behavior. It is not until later that frustration, natural adolescent rebellion, and anger combine to provide the courage needed for aggressive confrontation. Hostile behavior is perhaps the most effective means of escape through alienation in that it usually results in the victim's physically leaving the abusive family. However, it too leaves emotional scars which will adversely affect the victim's adjustment in adult life.

Should the victim of sexual abuse not find any of the methods just discussed to be effective in escaping, it is not at all unusual for her to seek a chemical escape. While the use of alcohol and other drugs does not appear to be as common among victims in Christian homes, they are occasionally resorted to in desperation. However, as we have seen already in our discussion of the damaged goods syndrome, drug and alcohol abuse are very common among victims of sexual abuse in the general population. Suffice it to say that in homes where substance abuse is an acceptable means of escaping other pressures, it is only logical that alcohol and drugs be used by the victim in coping with the pressures of sexual abuse as well.

Another more direct means of dealing with the problem of sexual abuse is simply removing oneself from the problem physically by running away. However, it has been my experience that running away from home is usually reserved by the victim as one of her last options. Thanks to the molester, she is convinced that it is her responsibility to hold the family together and, consequently, she is willing to let her own emotional needs go unmet rather than risk the destruction of the family. It is not until the burdens of tension, anger, disgust, and shame become unbearable that most victims will actually run away from home. The fact that sexual abuse is now one of the leading causes of runaways in the United States should be indicative of just how serious this problem is in our nation.

Closely related to running away is the practice of marrying as a means of escape. A victim will often marry at the first opportunity in an effort to physically leave the abusive environment—a common practice among incest victims. This usually occurs in the later teen years when the jealousy of the molester toward any boyfriends is felt most keenly and becomes the focal point of increasing conflicts. Such behavior could appropriately be likened to jumping out of the proverbial frying pan into the fire. As we shall discuss in chapter 6, such marriages often become nothing more than continuations of the abuse in a different setting and a means of passing this terrible heritage on to the next generation.

Where then, people ask, is there an effective and safe way for these children to escape their abuse? Surely if we can get them to report what is happening to the proper authorities, this madness can be stopped! Unfortunately, reporting the abuse, even in its early stages, is not always an effective means of stopping it. Although there has been a great deal of recent publicity and discussion on this subject, in most instances the public still deals with sexual abuse in ways that cause further emotional damage to the victim. Consequently, adults receiving reports of sexual abuse may ignore them. Poorly trained investigators often scare the child into silence, or the victim may be removed from the home rather than the offender, reinforcing the victim's feelings that the abuse is her fault. And let us not suppose that such things happen only in secular society. I have seen more than a few cases where children have reported sexual abuse to pastors or Sunday school teachers only to be told that "everything will be all right, I'm sure it won't happen again." Even those conscientious enough to investigate the child's story often take the molester's word, always accompanied by tears and repentance, that the offense will not recur.

Time and time again I have seen cases where young victims are humiliated, scared, and mistreated both by "the system" and by their own family members until they rescind their reports of abuse. I try not to think about the cases where we were forced to send an abused child back into her home knowing full well that she would continue to be molested. In such cases the victims are literally condemned to years of continued abuse and fear. And, having experienced the futility of reporting, it is unlikely these children will ever again seek outside help.

It is little wonder that some victims, with nothing to look forward to but years of humiliation, turn to suicide as the ultimate means of escape. To a child burdened by overwhelming responsibilities, guilt, self-hatred, and fear, suicide can appear to be a very desirable option. Many girls choose to sacrifice their own lives rather than destroy their family or continue to be subjected to sexual abuse.

When one considers the lengths to which these children go to stop what is happening to them, it becomes inconceivable that anyone would even dare to suggest that sexual abuse of children is "not all that harmful" and that we who are attempting to deal with this problem are overreacting. It is imperative that we as concerned human beings in general and as dedicated Christians in particular do everything in our power to help these innocent children escape from their victimization. It is equally important that we help to heal the damage already done and that we work to prevent the victimization of future generations by educating ourselves and acting in accordance with our knowledge.

CHAPTER SIX

The Iniquity of
the Fathers

It is a spiritual principle and a fact of human development that our actions as parents can and do affect our children and, through them, future generations. In Exodus 34:6-7 God makes it clear that our actions do not only affect us, but can have negative effects on our children and our children's children "to the third and the fourth generation." God's admonition to Moses in these verses was made specifically in regard to the sins of the fathers, which seems appropriate, considering our present subject matter.

Incest is an evil which not only affects the victim during the course of her victimization, but it haunts her for the rest of her life, often reproducing itself for generations. In this chapter we will consider the more long-term effects of child sexual abuse and some different ideas on why and how sexual abuse perpetuates itself. While all the data is by no means in on this subject and we can only speculate on how all this information fits together, an effort at understanding must be made for the sake of our children.

Emotional Fallout

During the Vietnam conflict, thousands of Americans lost their lives over a period of years. Yet, as tragic as those deaths were, they represent only a fraction of the damage done both to those directly involved and to their families. Our society is only now coming to grips with the residual, long-term effects of that conflict. It is estimated that since the United States pulled out of Vietnam, nearly three times as many veterans of that war have lost their lives through suicide as were actually killed on the battlefield. The toll in human misery and continuing emotional problems, both for veterans and their families, is incalculable. Thus, the most extensive damage done to our nation as the result of Vietnam has not been felt until years after the action itself was concluded.

Child sexual abuse in general, and incest in particular, seem to follow a similar pattern. Some of their most devastating effects are not felt until years after the abuse itself has been terminated. Recently, the American public has heard a lot about the phenomenon known as *post-traumatic stress disorder* in connection with Vietnam veterans. This term is often used when discussing the cause of certain peculiar behaviors and symptoms sometimes displayed by these veterans. The flashbacks and nightmares often accompanying this disorder have been the subject of many movies and television programs in recent years.

It has only lately been recognized that victims of sexual abuse often display many of the same symptoms observed in cases of post-traumatic stress disorder among veterans. Similarities in the causative factors behind these symptoms have also been observed. One clinical handbook states that this particular disorder results from a "psychologically traumatic event that is generally outside the range of usual human experience."[9] Such an event or series of events may be experienced by individuals or groups. They may result from the actions of other human beings, such as is the case with combat, bombings, torture, and rape. Or they may be the result of natural forces, as is the case with floods and earthquakes. From what we know of this problem, the emotional damage done to an individual tends to be more severe and long-lasting when the traumatic event was instigated by another human being. Child sexual abuse definitely fits that category.

One aspect of post-traumatic stress disorder which seems often to be present in cases of child sexual abuse is the tendency for the victim to mentally relive the experience or experiences which traumatized her. These memories tend to be intrusive—that is, they forcefully project themselves into the mind, often being triggered by something the victim has seen or heard. They may present themselves while the victim is awake and alert or may intrude on the victim's sleep in the form of a recurrent nightmare.

Recurring nightmares are common among sexual abuse victims and tend to continue until the problem is emotionally resolved. One woman in our treatment group reported that she was still being plagued with such reminders of her abuse even though the last actual incident had occurred nearly sixty years before. She is now seventy-four years of age and is still suffering from the effects of her victimization.

Other symptoms of post-traumatic stress disorder are a diminished ability to respond to other people—called *psychic numbing* or *emotional anesthesia*—and a partial or total inability to feel various emotions, especially those associated with intimacy and sexuality. The victim may also understandably attempt to avoid any activities or circumstances that tend to remind her of the trauma she suffered. This is one of the reasons it is often very difficult to get victims of sexual abuse to attend counseling voluntarily. Obviously, in the course of therapy the victim will be reminded repeatedly of her molestation and the pain that it caused her.

Whether or not child sexual abuse actually results in the victim experiencing post-traumatic stress disorder, the end results seem to be much the same and equally destructive. The psychic numbing mentioned usually interferes with interpersonal relationships, especially in marriage and family interaction. Also, guilt and depression usually lead to self-abusive behavior and sometimes even suicide, as discussed in chapter 5. Regardless of the label we give the emotional fallout caused by child sexual abuse, the damage is usually extensive and long-term. Until it is dealt with specifically by the victim, it will continue to cloud every important area of her life.

A Victim's Identity

After years of sexual exploitation and schooling in guilt and self-hatred, the victim of sexual abuse often develops what I refer to as a *victim's identity*. Something changes in her personality, her body language, and even sometimes her physical appearance. While this identity is not obvious to the average individual, it is quickly detected by those who tend to take advantage of weakness in others. Some criminals relate that simply by observing an individual for a few moments, they are able to determine whether or not that person will be an easy victim.

Unfortunately, with at least one of every four female children in our nation having been sexually abused, it appears there will be a steady supply of victims for some time to come. The ideal solution to this problem is total prevention of sexual abuse. However, we are aware that this is an impossible task. The best we can hope for is that through prayer, intercession, and education we can prevent many of these instances of abuse from occurring. And perhaps at the same time, we can learn how to understand and work with those who do fall victim to this evil.

Human behavior is a tremendously complex science, and factors that influence behavior are difficult to understand, fully known only to God our Creator. Although there are no simple explanations for human behavior, self-image seems to play a very important part in determining an individual's reactions. Understanding the principles of self-image can help explain some of the behavior patterns exhibited by victims of child sexual abuse.

Most so-called experts on human behavior agree that an individual's self-image is one of the most important factors in determining how that individual will adjust to his or her environment. How we feel about ourselves influences how we relate to others and how they relate to us. Everything we experience in life seems to be filtered through and influenced by our self-image. If we have a poor opinion of ourselves, we interpret the world around us from a negative perspective. We do not feel worthy of any good, and so we discard encouragement or praise because we feel we don't deserve it.

As Christians, we often find that a negative self-image even affects our relationship with God. We refuse his love and encouragement because we are basically no good. We insult God's provision for our forgiveness and happiness and instead stubbornly hang on to our negative self-image, using it as a tool for self-condemnation. It becomes difficult for us to see ourselves as God sees us, through the eyes of Christ, who has made each of us a new creature (2 Cor. 5:17). In other words, the bad feelings we have about ourselves make it possible for us not only to reject anything good that comes our way but even to seek punishment from other people or from God because we think we deserve it. Even though such self-abusive tendencies are not conscious, they are nevertheless extremely effective in producing pain and guilt.

Victims of child sexual abuse are even more drastically influenced by this tendency because of the conditioning they received while being molested. The constant input from the molester, who wanted his secret kept, slowly and solidly convinced the victim of her guilt. The shame that somehow she is to blame for what happened to her is an enduring shame that accompanies her as she grows up, leaves her home, and begins a family of her own. She is convinced she does not deserve happiness, loving children, or a supportive partner. Her belief in her own guilt is so strong that it blinds her even to the vulnerability of her children.

Professionals in this field are very familiar with cases in which a previous victim of incest will allow her father to care for her children only to learn later that he has molested them as well. When these women were asked why they exposed their children to the same person who molested them, they often responded by saying that they felt their children were good children who had done nothing wrong and therefore were not in danger of being molested. These mothers were totally convinced that their own abuse as children was due to the fact that they were worthless individuals or had somehow done something to deserve what had happened to them. But they considered their children to be worthwhile and therefore not in danger of abuse. Such convictions set the stage for the continued victimization of these mothers and the future abuse of their children as the sexual abuse cycle is repeated.

Marital Difficulties

One area in which the consequences of child sexual abuse are clearly seen is the various marital difficulties often experienced by those who have been victims. Such difficulties may begin at an early age as the victim attempts to escape her abuser by leaving home and getting married. Unfortunately, these victims often establish relationships with partners who will reinforce their negative self-images by continuing to abuse them in one form or another. And although this abuse may be physical rather than sexual in nature, it is just as effective in maintaining their pattern of victimization.

It is one thing to understand intellectually how the victim's identity and poor self-image combine to cause continued victimization. However, those of us working in this field cannot help but be amazed when we see a previous victim who chooses four or five different partners over a period of as many years and manages each time to find someone who both physically abuses her and sexually abuses her children. Admittedly, her behavior in these relationships may in some way encourage such abuse, but these men would have to be inclined to such abuse before they could follow through with it. How, we ask ourselves, do these people find each other so consistently? Unfortunately, we have not been able to come up with an answer to this riddle. All we know is that, whatever the process, it could not be more effective were they to take out classified ads in the local newspaper.

Linda was sexually abused as a child. She is now thirty-five years of age and has three children, two girls and a boy. Some time ago, Linda's oldest daughter, then eight, reported that Linda's common-law husband had tried to involve her in sexual activity. Linda was present when this man asked her daughter to orally copulate him and was even invited to encourage her daughter's cooperation. Linda agreed that her husband's behavior was not acceptable. However, when the case was thrown out of court because the judge did not consider what happened to be sexual abuse, she immediately resumed her relationship with this man. Her daughter continued to be molested by her partner, who felt he had received the sanction of the court to educate his stepdaughter.

After a number of months in this situation, Linda moved out of the area, saying she was tired of being physically abused. Unfortunately, within a matter of days of her move, Linda had met and begun living with a man who physically misused her and sexually abused both of her daughters. Linda stayed in that situation for a considerable length of time, leaving this man only after a year and a half of abuse when he began serving his prison term for molesting her daughters. It turned out that Linda had chosen a partner with a previous history of child sexual abuse.

Linda then moved back and almost immediately began living with a previously convicted sex offender. To make a long story short, it was less than a year before her new boyfriend was also serving time for sexual abuse. On top of all this, Linda then decided that she still loved her first common-law husband and consequently moved back in with him. Interestingly enough, Linda had not been aware of the past problems of any of her partners in the area of sexual abuse until each was accused of molesting her children.

Most cases of inappropriate partner choice are not as severe as Linda's. But many contain some of the same elements on a smaller scale. A previous victim with unmet dependency needs chooses a partner hoping she will find the nurturing father she never had. She makes the mistake of interpreting aggression as strength of character and only manages to continue her victimization.

Another previous victim may choose a passive, emotionally immature partner so she can continue her role as mother. In either case, when the additional factors of guilt and low self-image come into play, the result is a potential sexually abusive family. This is especially true if the partner of choice has himself been molested as a child, which is often the case.

Even for the lucky ones who manage to find reasonably well-adjusted partners who will not molest their children, there are other difficulties to face as the result of their previous victimization. Sexual adjustment problems, many of which can be categorized as serious, are almost universal among previous victims of continued sexual abuse. Such problems range from a simple confusion of love and sex to complete frigidity. Many of these women find that any sexual activity is repulsive to them. Sexual contact is avoided whenever possible and, when unavoidable, is treated as a nuisance, to be endured and dispensed with as quickly as possible. To such women, the concept of experiencing pleasure in sexual interaction is unthinkable.

Other women who have experienced sexual abuse as children report alternating between periods of relatively satisfactory sexual experiences and periods of revulsion and great emotional distress. They may revert to using sex as a means of getting attention from or manipulating their partners and usually experience condemning guilt when they do so. Others report that they enjoy their sexual relationships with their partners most of the time. However, on occasion something their partner does or says will remind them of their molester and a flashback will put an abrupt end to any intimacy, at least for the time being.

For those previous victims fortunate enough to have met an understanding, stable partner, these sexual problems may be nothing more than obstacles to sexual adjustment that often respond to appropriate counseling. For those not so fortunate, such problems often foretell the end of their marriage and the beginning of unspeakable misery for their children.

Child-Rearing Problems

Just as important as the choice of partners in the causative cycle of child sexual abuse are the child-rearing practices of the previous victim. Such practices are heavily influenced by the conditioning the victim receives as a child. Without being aware of what is happening, she may inadvertently set her children up to be sexually abused by her husband or another trusted adult. Though her intentions may be good, she has usually been so scarred by her own experiences as a child that it becomes impossible for her to be objective and well-balanced in raising her children.

The initial stages of child-rearing may go smoothly in some of these families, and mother-child relationships may be perfectly normal at first. However, in many such families, even this early period is problem-ridden because of an unrealistic expectation on the part of the mother. She wants her child to be a sweet, cuddly baby showing her love and not demanding anything in return. But these mothers quickly learn that babies have needs and demands of their own and seem to care little about what their mothers want or need. In such instances, rejection of the child may begin early and may even result in physical abuse.

Even in cases where the first few years of child-rearing do proceed smoothly, it is often not long before the mother begins to duplicate the patterns that existed in her family as a child. As her daughter gets older, the mother may begin to confide in her as if she were an adult. Their relationship at first may seem better and open. Soon her daughter is listening to her problems and even providing emotional support. At the same time the daughter may develop the same kind of relationship with her father or father figure.

As the daughter approaches the age at which her mother was first molested, her mother's memories of that molestation often increase in frequency and severity. The daughter may remind her of herself when she was a child. Such recollections become increasingly painful for the previous victim and, without realizing it, she begins to withdraw emotionally from her daughter. Communication slowly fades. At the same time the previous victim is suffering from these painful memories, her husband does not understand what is happening and expects their sexual relationship to continue as before—even if it was not the best. However, memories of her victimization and visions of the adult male who took advantage of her may cause this mother to completely discontinue sexual relations with her partner. Or, she may subconsciously make them such an unpleasant experience for him that he grudgingly decreases his sexual advances.

With the mother's gradual withdrawal as an emotional support within the family, the other family members begin to seek support elsewhere. The daughter, finding herself deprived of a relationship with her mother, may spend more time in her father's company. Often, she has already begun to provide some of his emotional support, and now that both father and daughter are feeling abandoned, they tend to seek encouragement from one another. Since these fathers seldom have the emotional maturity necessary to confront such issues head on, they cannot bring themselves to make an effort at resolving the communication and sexual problems with their wives. It is much easier to turn to the innocent, non-judgmental companionship of their daughters, who seem always to be available and trusting.

As this process continues, father and daughter are drawn closer by the dynamics of dependency. At first, their relationship is mutually supportive and comforting. Unfortunately, because of the emotional shortcomings often seen in these men, they tend to be unable to draw a distinction between love and sex. As the mother relinquishes her role within the family and the daughter takes it up out of necessity, her father begins to relate to her more as a wife than a daughter. The initiation of sexual activity in such a relationship is gradual and may be perceived by the immature father as an expression of his love for his daughter. However, as discussed earlier, such behavior is seen in a completely different light by his victim.

Once the abuse has begun, the secret of incest takes over the whole family, ruining relationships and causing division and tension. The cycle continues as the new incest victim eventually leaves the home emotionally scarred and heading toward relationships of her own—in which this problem will continue to grow and reproduce. Somewhere down the line, perhaps somebody will seek help in breaking this evil chain of events that threatens the very existence of the family in our society.

The process I have just described can take many different forms. As already stated, there are no simple explanations of or solutions to the problem of child sexual abuse. The basic elements are usually the same but the exact circumstances and the cast of players have innumerable variations. What is important to understand is that the biggest danger of child sexual abuse is its tendency to reproduce itself. And the only effective way to stop its reproduction is to interfere with the sexual abuse cycle.

Homosexual Orientation

So far in this chapter we have discussed the long-term effects that child sexual abuse has on the victim's emotional development and self-image, her relationship with her partner, and her relationship with her children. Another area I would like to cover at this point appears not to be of major significance as far as the number of individuals affected. However, it is of considerable moral significance and is an issue which often surfaces in the treatment of this problem. As such it should be dealt with.

In some cases of sexual abuse, especially long-term incestuous relationships, the abuse may have the residual effect of changing the victim's sexual orientation. By this I mean that these victims may find themselves being drawn toward bisexual or homosexual tendencies as a result of their victimization. From my experience and that of others in the field with whom I have talked, this seems more often to be the case in instances where the victim herself regards her abuse as having been particularly traumatic and damaging. It also seems to be more common in cases where there have been multiple experiences of victimization by the opposite sex even after the victim had escaped from the initial abuse within her home.

While it is my personal belief, based on such Scriptures as 1 Corinthians 6:9–10, that homosexual activity cannot be morally justified, I can also understand how victims of sexual abuse are influenced in that direction. In most instances of abuse the molester is a member of the opposite sex, which puts two strikes against the offending gender. The more serious and long-term the molestation is, the more resentment and hatred are built up against the molester and, by association, against all those of the molester's sex. Even after the victim escapes the initial environment of abuse, she often begins a series of relationships with other abusive men. She does not realize that because of the dynamics of child sexual abuse, her initial victimization has negatively influenced her choice of partners. Consequently, these experiences tend to reinforce her negative opinion of the opposite sex.

Combined with the victim's building mistrust of men may be a longing for female nurturing, nurturing she did not receive within her family. Also, as she begins to deal with the problems caused by her molestation, the people to whom she turns for support are often other women who may have had similar experiences. She does not feel threatened by them, as they are usually sympathetic and understanding. Neither does she feel concerned about being sexually exploited by them. To some of these victims, especially those who have no contrary moral beliefs, it seems an easy transition from mutual emotional support to sexual involvement.

In her book on father-daughter incest, Judith Herman relates two studies which indicate a connection between child sexual abuse and the development of a lesbian identity. In one study, over a third of the incest victims interviewed reported having developed a lesbian orientation. In another, a national survey of lesbians indicated that a significantly greater number of these women had experienced child sexual abuse than had the women in the heterosexual control group. Herman herself reports not having found any such connection in her survey of incest victims. However, she does state that two of the forty victims in her study had developed a confirmed lesbian identity and that three others considered themselves bisexual.[10] These five individuals constituted 12.5 percent of the total population of her study. While such a percentage does not by any means indicate a major trend among incest victims, it does seem to me to be indicative of some causative relationship between incest and sexual orientation.

Psychosis

The last subject we will consider in our discussion of the effects of child sexual abuse constitutes the ultimate escape mechanism available to the abuse victim outside of suicide. Psychosis, or mental illness, seems to be encountered mainly among individuals who have been victims in the more "serious" cases of child sexual abuse. In the instances of which I am aware from personal experience, the abuser was usually the victim's natural father. The abuse itself tended to be long term and to contain elements of sadism and violence or threats of violence. In other words, the emotional damage done appeared to be exaggerated by the level of trust being betrayed and the extreme degree to which the abuse had been carried.

Few of these cases seem to have happy endings. The prognosis for recovery among such victims is unusually poor. One case I am aware of ended in the suicide of the victim. Even her psychosis did not provide enough of an escape. In another, the victim is even now wandering from town to town, exposing her daughter to sexual abuse as she attempts to exist in a fantasy world. Yet another victim is confined to a mental institution, her behavior considered too violent to be controlled, even through psychotropic drugs. It is this last case which causes me the most distress as a professional and which I would like to share with you. Perhaps it will provide some insight into the long-term damage done by sexual abuse.

> Louise is the forty-year-old daughter of a hard-working, lower-middle-class laborer now approaching his seventieth birthday. Her family moved to California some thirty years ago and has since been residing on a secluded ranch in the northern part of the state. Louise and her younger sister have been sexually abused by their father since they were very young, so young that neither can remember the age at which it all began.
>
> Louise's sister Sharon, who is now thirty-six, was a very timid child when the abuse began and did not resist her father's sexual advances. Louise was not so timid. She did resist, at one point even threatening to tell a teacher about the abuse. Her father threatened to kill her if she ever told anyone, and after a few well-timed beatings, Louise knew he meant business. She finally resigned herself to living with her victimization.
>
> As the two girls grew up, the abuse continued. Louise's father was partial to Sharon. She received special privileges and gifts from her father and he never struck her, as far as Louise could recall. His relationship with Louise, however, was quite different. He never forgave her for her initial resistance. His sexual demands became increasingly bizarre and violent. Louise finally became so distraught that she tried to tell her mother about the abuse. Her mother became very angry, slapped her face, and told Louise that she was a liar and was never to repeat her story to anyone else.

After years of abuse, the pressure eventually became too much for Louise and she was found one day wandering along a highway many miles from home, babbling incoherently. Her parents quickly admitted her to a mental institution. In the years since her first admission, Louise has been released on a number of occasions and sent home to live with her parents. Each time the sexual abuse resumed, and each time Louise would have to be readmitted to the hospital after a psychotic episode.

One day during Louise's last furlough, her mother heard screams coming from the cabin in which Louise stayed when she was home. She ran the short distance to the cabin from the main house to find her husband in Louise's bedroom, clad only in his underwear. Louise was clawing at him and screaming at the top of her lungs. When her mother arrived, Louise's father immediately began accusing Louise of trying to seduce him. He claimed that she had demanded that he undress and lie down on her bed and that he had complied out of fear of what she might do to him. Louise by this time was so distraught that she could do nothing but run from the cabin screaming. Her mother agreed that it was obviously best for Louise to return to the hospital in order to protect her father from any further attack.

It came to our attention not long after this incident that Louise's father had also molested his sons as they were growing up and had in recent years been sexually abusing five of his grandchildren. To this day he continues to molest Sharon, who has never married. Unfortunately, these family members were so intimidated by this man and his control of the family was so tight that we were unable to get enough evidence to stop the abuse. Stories were changed under family pressure or denied altogether and the investigation came to a grinding halt. Now, each time I pass that ranch, I can't help but think of the children still being molested who are beyond our reach and of Louise, again confined to a mental institution.

Yes, I believe that psychosis does result from child sexual abuse in some instances. Louise's family and others like it actually do exist. And, of all the types of child sexual abuse cases, these are among the most heartbreaking since no one seems to know how to treat these victims effectively. Even treatment in the average case of child sexual abuse is a tricky undertaking, but when the situation is compounded by psychosis, the treatment problems are multiplied enormously. Let us pray that we are successful in our efforts to control this problem before it results in too many more of these cases.

——————— CHAPTER SEVEN ———————

Take It Like a Man

Up to this point in the book we have been considering the dynamics of child sexual abuse mainly as they apply to the female victim. This is partially due to the fact that female victims, according to the statistics available to us at this point, are more numerous than male victims. Also, since more studies have been conducted in regard to female victims, more is known about the dynamics of their abuse.

While the study of child sexual abuse in general is a comparatively new field, the specific study of the male victim is a frontier only now being challenged. Very few studies have been done on this problem and few treatment programs have been developed to address it. Consequently, there are few experts on the subject and little data on which to base solid conclusions.

Unfortunately, the whole subject of child sexual abuse among males has been basically ignored by our society. Although the reasons for such an attitude are not really clear at this point, what is clear is that male victims of sexual abuse are suffering because of it. It is also clear, as we shall see in this chapter, that if we hope to make any effective progress toward eliminating child sexual abuse, we must spend more time seeking solutions to the unique problems presented by the male victim.

An Under-Reported Problem

Statistical information on the sexual abuse of male children is sparse, to say the least. However, by combining what data we do have with the personal observations of those treating male victims, we can get some idea of the nature and scope of this problem. It should be pointed out that underreporting is even more of a problem among male victims of sexual abuse than among female victims. Therefore, statistics representing actual reports of abuse constitute only a small fraction of those actually being victimized and should be considered extremely conservative indicators of the actual occurrence of this problem.

Until very recently the phenomenon of sexual abuse among male children in the United States was thought to be extremely rare. Estimates of such abuse seem to have followed the same general pattern of reporting seen in the study of father-daughter incest. When first studied seriously in the 1950s, it was estimated that there were only one or two incest victims for every million people in the nation. As more accurate studies were conducted, that figure was revised upward to forty victims per million in the late 1960s and then to one thousand cases per million by the late 1970s. Studies done in the last few years have surpassed even those figures, and the trend continues upward as public education improves.

Estimates on the incidence of sexual abuse among male children vary widely. Some propose that girls are victims of molestation ten times as often as boys. Others estimate that girls are victimized only twice as often. Some even propose that the rate of victimization is equal. In Finkelhor's study of college students in 1979, he found that 9 percent of the male students surveyed reported having been sexually abused as children.[11] Another study done about the same time in a large hospital showed that 25 percent of its child sexual abuse victims were male.[12]

Other studies indicate even higher figures on the molestation of male children. A recent report by the District Attorney's Office in Hennepin County, Minnesota, showed that boys in the country's lower grades of elementary school were just as likely to report sexual abuse as were girls in the same grade levels.[13] Elsewhere, in a study of 1,800 college students, almost a third of both sexes reported having been victims of sexual abuse as children. What is even more disturbing is the fact that half of the female students reporting abuse had told their parents of their victimization, but only one tenth of the male victims had done so.[14]

A Deeper Secret

It is the extreme reluctance of male sexual abuse victims to report their abuse which seems more than any other factor to distinguish them from their female counterparts. While we have pointed out the fact that female children are very hesitant to report their victimization, their reluctance fades in comparison to that of the male victim. There are several reasons for the male victim's resistance to reporting sexual abuse. They tend to be the same reasons that society often ignores the sexual abuse of boys, even when it is reported.

In our culture, and indeed in many cultures, boys are taught that the essence of masculinity is the ability to protect oneself. Masculinity means being self-sufficient, strong, and aggressive. In other words, it means not being a victim. Our society does not allow males to express helplessness or vulnerability. Those who do express such feelings are usually considered weak and often become targets for abuse by their peers. Boys learn these lessons early through everything from the toys they play with to the roles portrayed by their heroes on television. The message given is strong and clear, leaving very little room for interpretation. Even many Christian families promote such ideals among their children in direct contradiction to the Word of God, which tells us that God's power is made perfect in our weakness (2 Cor. 12:9), and that a gentle and quiet spirit is very precious in God's sight (1 Peter 3:4).

Boys learn that it is not acceptable for a male to be a victim. Victimization indicates a defect in masculinity, in the ability to protect oneself. On the other hand, boys are taught through the same types of mechanisms that a female can be victim and still maintain her sexual identity. This sexual double standard manifests itself in the different reporting ratios for male and female victims of child sexual abuse.

When a girl is sexually abused, she is considered defiled or somehow damaged and in need of emotional repair through counseling. However, if a boy is sexually abused, he is expected to "take it like a man." It is not acceptable for him to be emotionally damaged without it reflecting on his masculinity. Besides, girls are not expected to enjoy sexual activity for some reason and boys are. It is not considered normal for a boy to object to sexual involvement, especially if that involvement is with an older female.

If a boy is molested by another male, an additional factor comes into play. Added to the issues of self-protection and aggression is the issue of homosexuality. The victim may fear that if he reports the abuse he will be labeled as a homosexual or, at the very least, people will wonder about that possibility. He will likely wonder himself whether what happened to him makes him a homosexual. This is a fear often encountered among male victims of child sexual abuse.

Unfortunately, the media does little to educate male children. Even with recent attempts to consider the subject of child sexual abuse, most coverage focuses on female incest cases and sensational criminal cases. The subject of male victimization might be mentioned only in passing during a news broadcast about sexual abuse in a day care facility. Victims of child sexual abuse are generally portrayed as female and most are interviewed as adults.

To the credit of a few networks, there has been some accurate material presented on children's programs recently. But much remains to be done in the area of enlightened programming. If the social conscience of the media runs true to form, it will undoubtedly be a long time before we see any significant improvement in this area. Meanwhile, male victims of sexual abuse do not see much evidence that these terrible things are happening to anyone else. Therefore, they often assume they must somehow be different or defective and consequently may deserve what happened to them. Add to this self-doubt the fear of being labeled a "sissy" or a "queer" and the result is a successful formula for silence and continued abuse.

A Different Kind of Victim

Male victims of child sexual abuse fall into two categories: those molested by a member of their own sex, and those molested by a member of the opposite sex. The effect that the molestation has on the victim will depend, to a great degree, on what sex the molester was and the relationship between victim and molester. These factors will be discussed shortly. However, before we consider the differences between the two classifications of male victims, it might be useful to look at how male victims differ statistically from female victims. Keep in mind that these are general differences and don't apply to all cases.

First of all, male victims are more likely to be sexually abused by someone outside of the family than are female victims. Tied closely with this characteristic is another finding that male sexual abuse victims are also more likely to be from single-parent families. What seems to happen in many of these cases is that the victim's father is either absent from the home or the father-son relationship within the home is poor. Because of the lack of this vital relationship, these boys are often involved in a perpetual search for a father figure. It is a search which leaves them vulnerable to molesters, who are experts at gaining the confidence of children and involving them in sexual activity. It is obvious from the criminal statistics that such methods are effective. Some specific methods used by these molesters will be discussed in chapter 11.

Another general characteristic of male sexual abuse victims is that they are more likely to be abused by someone of the same sex than are female victims. Several attempts have been made to explain why females in our society are less likely to molest someone of their own sex than are males. Some claim that females are less sexually aggressive in our culture because of social conditioning aimed at making them more nurturing and submissive. While I definitely feel that such social conditioning is a factor in this matter, I also believe that other factors such as the biological and emotional differences between men and women should be taken into consideration. Furthermore, I cannot help but feel that the woman who carries and gives birth to a child is much less likely to victimize that child, even if all other factors were equal.

Male victims of sexual abuse are also more likely to be physically abused as well as sexually abused by their molesters. This tendency could account for the fact that the highest ratios of boy victims to girl victims in sexual abuse cases have been reported by law enforcement agencies and hospitals. These two institutions are the ones most likely to be aware of physical injuries sustained by children. Also, since male victims tend to be molested by people outside their families, one would assume that these molesters would be more likely to resort to physical force.

These statistical characteristics of male victims are useful to some extent in getting a general picture of the differences between male and female victims of child sexual abuse. However, the next two subject headings will deal with important specific factors influencing male victims.

Sexual Identity Crisis

From the information available to us at this point, it seems clear that boys, like girls, are most commonly victimized by men.[15] When a male child is molested by an older member of the same sex, that child suffers from many of the same problems evident among female victims of child sexual abuse. Feelings of fear, confusion, guilt, and helplessness are experienced for much the same reasons that they are experienced by the female victim. Betrayal is also acutely experienced where the molester is a parent or other adult with whom the child has developed a relationship of trust.

To varying degrees, depending on the circumstances of the molestation and the background of the child, the male victim may also experience grief over the loss of his sexual innocence. This problem, however, seems to be more acute among female victims. Another feeling usually present to one degree or another is anger or bitterness toward the molester for what he has done, even though that anger seems often not to be uncovered until treatment is under way. Disruption of family stability and peer relationships may also be observed when males are victimized in homosexual encounters.

One of the most serious effects of this type of molestation is the confusion the victim experiences in regard to his sexual identity. This phenomenon could be regarded as a modified form of the *damaged goods syndrome* seen in female victims. With the very first instance of molestation, a feeling of total confusion comes over the male victim. Although he cannot understand why this happened to him, he is usually well aware of society's views on such actions and how they reflect on the issue of masculinity. And, just as is the case with female victims, he feels that the abuse must have been caused by something he did or by what kind of person he is. Male victims often ask themselves if they could somehow be homosexual without knowing it and if the molester might somehow have sensed this and been attracted to them.

On top of all this confusion, yet another question presents itself to the victim. "Even if I was not a homosexual before, does what happened to me make me a homosexual?" As ridiculous as such a question may seem, it is a very common concern among boys who are victims of sexual abuse. In fact, even adult male victims of homosexual rape often report having had the same concern. Unfortunately, because the male victim is so afraid of being labeled a homosexual and losing his masculine identity, he often decides not to report his abuse. These boys, then, are often forced to deal with their emotional turmoil alone in the best way they know how, just like their female counterparts. But the added issues of masculinity and homosexuality make it even less likely that they will seek help.

Unrealistic Expectations

As mentioned earlier in this chapter, there is another major category of male child sexual abuse victims which needs to be considered. That category includes all male children sexually abused by female molesters. Such abuse may be perpetrated by the child's caretaker, his mother, another relative, or any number of other females having access to him. These cases are less often encountered than are those just described, at least as far as reporting statistics are concerned. Unfortunately, in addition to being one of the least common forms of child sexual abuse, it is also perhaps the least understood.

Very few cases of sexual abuse in this category are reported and even fewer are in treatment. When such cases do come to light, the duplistic attitudes prevalent in our society regarding this problem become evident with the result that an extreme disservice is done to the male child victim. By looking at two of these attitudes, perhaps we can get a clearer understanding of what these victims face.

First of all, there exists within our society a misconception that the seduction of a male child is probably a positive experience for that child. After all, we are taught that males are supposed to enjoy sexual activity with members of the opposite sex, regardless of the circumstances. How could a boy be harmed by such a pleasurable experience? This "red-blooded American boy" syndrome brings into question the masculinity of any male child who appears uncomfortable with sexual contact initiated by an older member of the opposite sex.

Closely related is the myth of the romantic initiation in our society. This myth has become, as it were, a national sexual fantasy among adult males and as such is jealously guarded and carefully perpetuated. It is most commonly seen in the entertainment world, woven into the plots of such films as *The Last Picture Show* and *Honky Tonk Man*. Wherever it is seen in our society, this myth portrays boy-woman sex as a romantic initiation into manhood. Almost always such activity is portrayed as a positive and fulfilling experience, both for the boy who has learned the joys of manhood and for the woman who was able to contribute to his education.

The real truth is that neither of these wishful delusions bears any resemblance to the reality of what happens when a boy is molested by a woman. These victims suffer from the same massive confusion, fear, guilt, and helplessness experienced by children in the other categories of child sexual abuse already discussed. Their feelings of confusion are often intensified by the fact that their molester was a female—someone they had been taught to view as nurturing and supportive, not predatory and selfish.

Anyone questioning the harm done to a boy in such a situation need only visit a treatment group in which these boys are discussing their victimization. It is difficult to maintain myths and fantasies when face to face with the reality of damaged children.

Mother-Child Incest: The Ultimate Betrayal

Among boys who have been molested by adults there exists a small number who warrant some special consideration. This group consists of boys who have been sexually molested by their mothers or mother surrogates. Professionals working with these children have found that the emotional damage done in such cases of mother-child incest seems often to be greater than that found in any other category of child sexual abuse. Again, without more data, it is difficult to come to any firm conclusions. However, therapists treating victims of mother-child incest report especially severe emotional damage among their clients.

These victims suffer from most of the same problems attributed to other forms of child sexual abuse. In addition, they must face the terrible stigma of having been involved in the violation of society's strongest taboo, that of mother-child incest.

In relation to their children, mothers in our society are portrayed as non-sexual, nurturing individuals incapable of sexually abusing their children. Motherhood represents all that is good and wholesome in our society. Nevertheless, there is no denying the fact that some mothers do sexually abuse their children. As much of a blow as this may be to our cultural sensitivities, it is nothing in comparison to the emotional shock experienced by the victim.

Even though at the onset of this type of incest the victim may not be aware of society's attitude toward such activities, it is not long before he begins to realize the sacred place which mothers hold in the social order. As he becomes increasingly aware of the unacceptable nature of what is happening, the victim not only begins to experience undeserved guilt but often comes to believe that he must be especially evil or possibly even insane to have participated in such a terrible activity. Guilt over any physical pleasure he may have experienced during his molestation serves to compound his growing self-hatred, just as it does with the victim of father-daughter incest.

Some of the most disturbed individuals I have seen in my professional experience have been victims of this type of sexual abuse. I remember in particular one man who seemed to show up at every public education seminar which our department presented on child sexual abuse. He would usually arrive late and sit in the back of the room. When the presentation was almost complete, I could count on him to interrupt the program with a passionate and angry speech on the fact that mothers as well as fathers molest their children.

I could not help but feel sorry for this man despite the disruptions he caused. One day he came into my office weeping bitterly and poured out his heart to me, relating how he had been molested by his mother as a boy and how he had also spent time in prison for sexually molesting his daughter. The disturbance caused in this man's life and the lives of those around him by what his mother did has been severe and debilitating. In fact, I have just learned that he was recently convicted of sexually abusing a young girl for whom he was caretaker.

Few professionals would argue with the fact that mother-child incest tends to have an especially serious effect on the emotional lives of the victims. Several studies have even indicated this type of abuse as a possible causative factor in violent crimes against women. Even though mother-child incest seems to be much less prevalent than other forms of child sexual abuse in our nation, we must not allow ourselves to ignore its victims in any way.

The Victim as Victimizer

Perhaps the most important single difference we see between the effects of child sexual abuse on female victims and those on male victims is the tendency of the male victim to become a victimizer. It is becoming increasingly clear as we study this problem that the female victim tends to victimize herself as the result of having been sexually abused. Her negative self-image, developed as the result of her molestation, is acted out in such a way as to invite others to punish her for what she perceives as her own shortcomings. Consequently, histories of self-abusive behavior in the form of sexual promiscuity, substance abuse, prostitution, and choice of abusive marital partners are common among female victims. This phenomenon is due to a combination of factors including societal conditioning in general and conditioning within the family in particular.

Even though the social climate within our nation has been changing in recent years, the general message to female children to this point has been consistent. Girls have been taught that a nurturing personality is a desirable characteristic in females. At the same time, aggression has been discouraged as not being compatible with such a personality. In addition to these societal messages, the female incest victim is conditioned within the family unit itself that her primary role is nurturing, however warped that family's particular viewpoint of nurturing might be.

Female incest victims are trained and expected to meet the sexual and emotional needs of their fathers—and often the emotional needs of their mothers as well. In many cases they are also expected to act as a nurturing parent to their siblings and are made to feel responsible for the care, sometimes even the existence, of their families. When an incest victim is faced with her own frustration and anger at what has happened to her, it is likely that because of her conditioning she will turn that anger on herself, rather than on those whom she has been taught to nurture and protect.

It should be pointed out here that the conditioning of female children in our society to be nurturing is not the problem. Nurturing is not in and of itself an undesirable characteristic—quite to the contrary. We as Christians are admonished in numerous instances throughout the New Testament to develop and treasure such attributes. We are told in Philippians 2:4 that we should consider the interests of others before we consider our own. In other Scriptures we are told to pray for one another, uphold one another, and even to provide for the physical needs of those around us. The problem is not in the principle of nurturing but in the distortion of God's design for it.

God has made it plain to us through his Word that to be nurturing is a desirable characteristic for all people, whether male or female, child or adult. In fact, one of the most specific commands on this subject is addressed directly to men. In Ephesians 5:28–30, Paul makes clear the mind of God on this subject when he writes,

> Even so husbands should love their wives as their own bodies. He who loves his wife loves himself. For no man ever hates his own flesh, but nourishes and cherishes it, as Christ does the church, because we are members of his body.

Unfortunately, the male in our society is trained to be aggressive rather than caring or nurturing. And, I am ashamed to admit, we Christian men have often been influenced in this by the attitude of the world. Boys growing up in our culture are taught that aggression is better than concern and that only the weak express their feelings or allow themselves to be victimized. They learn that violence and aggression are the only manly answers to victimization. And they are taught that the best way to deal with being victimized and to regain control of their lives is to victimize or control someone else.

Is it any wonder then that male victims of child sexual abuse in our nation often grow up to inflict sexual abuse on others weaker than themselves? By abusing, they seek to gain control and to transfer their pain to another. What else can we expect as a society from children who have been trained in the overpowering law of survival through retaliation and aggression?

It is incumbent upon us as Christians to lead the way in training our children properly in the concepts of concern and nurturing. The Bible admonishes parents to "train up a child in the way he should go, and when he is old he will not depart from it" (Prov. 22:6). By training our children, both boys and girls, that concern and nurturing are desirable qualities, we can help lay the foundation for the prevention of victimization in future generations.

CHAPTER EIGHT

Whispers That Are Screams

Now that we are aware of the fact that child sexual abuse does take place and have seen the distastrous effects it can have, it is important that we learn to recognize the problem when we encounter it in individuals and families. Without recognition, intervention and treatment are obviously impossible.

A massive trauma such as child sexual abuse cannot be experienced by an individual or a family unit without causing certain symptoms to develop. Such symptoms fall into several general categories. These have been recognized and verified through the experience of hundreds of professionals working with thousands of sexual abuse victims and their families. Recognition of these symptoms makes early intervention possible, thus sparing the victim years of confusion and emotional turmoil and often saving a family from destruction.

There are three general categories of child sexual abuse indicators. The first includes specific behavior which suggests an individual has been the victim of sexual abuse. The second category consists of family characteristics which might be seen either in families at high risk or in those already involved in sexual abuse. And the third category deals with physical evidence considered to be indicative of child sexual abuse.

It should be kept in mind as we review these indicators of child sexual abuse that the presence of one or even several in a child or family is by no means conclusive proof of the existence of sexual abuse. The indicators listed are warning signals similar to medical symptoms useful in diagnosing illnesses. One or two such symptoms may simply spark a concern that leads to a closer investigation of the problem. The presence of yet another symptom gives a definite direction to the diagnostic process. And the presence of still another calls for clear and decisive action. A lot depends also on which symptom is presenting itself as to how important it is in reaching a conclusion. An x-ray is more likely to be conclusive evidence of a certain condition than is a vague pain alluded to by the patient.

In this chapter, I will be presenting several lists compiled from my personal experience and an extensive review of indicators listed by other professionals in the field. In these lists an effort has been made to group the most significant indicators of sexual abuse toward the top of each list. Such weighting of these indicators is not based on any scientific data but on personal observations of which indicators are encountered most frequently and which seem to be the most conclusive. However, in the particular case with which you may be concerned, an indicator at the end of a list might be as significant or more so than one at the beginning. For this reason I encourage each person reading this book to review the entire list in each category. Missing any of these indicators could mean unnecessary suffering for a child victim.

While the behavior and characteristics we will review in this chapter are by no means infallible indicators of sexual abuse, they have proven to be reliable tools in locating victims and their families. It is essential that such tools be available to the parents, friends, and counselors of these children since the victims themselves are effectively prevented from reporting in most cases by a conspiracy of silence. Besides, a molester rarely seeks help on his own to end child sexual abuse. It is therefore up to other concerned individuals to intervene on behalf of the child victim. But whether you are a conscientious parent or relative, a concerned friend, a pastor, or a professional counselor, you cannot help with a problem you are unable to recognize.

Behavioral Indicators

Of the three categories of child sexual abuse indicators, perhaps the most helpful in diagnosing this problem is that category dealing with individual behavior often observed in victims. Because of the secrecy and social isolation usually seen in these families, indicators in the other areas of family dynamics and physical clues are often not available for consideration.

Fortunately, most children in our nation attend school on a regular basis and are consequently observed by teachers who can play an important part in the detection of child sexual abuse. However, teachers to this point have had little, if any, training in how to recognize sexual abuse victims among their students. I am reminded of this unfortunate fact in nearly every school where I have given training sessions on this subject. Usually at least one teacher will approach me after the presentation and sadly relate the story of a previous student who had displayed clear indicators of having been sexually abused. Unfortunately, such students are usually out of reach by the time the teacher realizes what has been happening.

Behavioral indicators of child sexual abuse tend to vary according to the age of the victim and so will be dealt with in four age divisions. Sometimes an indicator listed in one age group will be observed in a child from a different age division. Please don't let any such overlapping bother you. What is important is that the behavior has been observed and should cause us to suspect the possibility of abuse. And even though the detection of sexual abuse is far from a science, these lists have proven to be very helpful in exposing this problem among children.

You will notice also that the fourth age division includes those behavioral indicators observed in adults. This section is included mainly for the benefit of counselors, pastoral or otherwise, who are working with adult clients. I can promise such counselors that if they question their clients with these indicators in mind, they will be shocked by the number who have been affected by this problem. They will also learn that much of the maladaptive behavior exhibited by such clients is directly related to their sexual victimization as children. A mental health therapist who recently sat through one of our presentations was flabbergasted by the number of sexual abuse victims he subsequently discovered among his female clients. Since that presentation, he has been the source of a constant stream of referrals to our agency.

Behavioral Indicators in Infants and Preschoolers: The first division we will discuss in the area of behavioral indicators includes children who fall into the age category of *infants and preschoolers.* Please remember that these age divisions are general categories and there are no precise age definitions for these terms, even among professionals in this field. For the purposes of this chapter, the division of infants and preschoolers will include children from birth through age five.

Many people have trouble believing that anyone would sexually abuse a child in this age category. Unfortunately, it is very common to encounter instances of child sexual abuse among such children. I have personally seen cases of sexual abuse involving victims who were only a few months old and have heard of others in which the victims were babies only a few days old. With increased public education and prevention programs within the community, we are seeing a marked increase in the number of referrals of children in this age division. This is encouraging in one sense, as it means that intervention can be attempted at an earlier age, thus sparing the victim many more years of abuse. It is also frustrating, as most three- and four-year-olds make terrible witnesses in a criminal justice system which has refused to make allowances for young victims.

Following is the list of behavioral indicators often observed among infants and preschoolers who have been sexually abused. After you have read the list, we will discuss a few of the more important indicators enumerated.

*Behavioral Indicators of Sexual Abuse
in Infants and Preschoolers*

1. Being uncomfortable around previously trusted persons
2. Sexualized behavior (excessive masturbation, sexually inserting objects, explicit sex play with other children, etc.)
3. Fear of restrooms, showers, or baths (common locations of abuse)
4. Fear of being alone with men or boys
5. Nightmares on a regular basis or about the same person
6. Abrupt personality changes
7. Uncharacteristic hyperactivity
8. Moodiness, excessive crying
9. Aggressive or violent behavior toward other children
10. Difficulty in sleeping or relaxing
11. Clinging behavior which may take the form of separation anxiety
12. Passive or withdrawn behavior

Most of the indicators in this list are self-explanatory and some will be recognized from material already covered in previous chapters. Note that the symptoms mentioned usually indicate the possibility of sexual abuse when they represent a change in the child's behavior. If a child has always been quiet and withdrawn or moody, the simple existence of those attributes may not be indicative of sexual abuse at all. However, if a normally cheerful child suddenly becomes withdrawn and begins crying at the slightest problem, a parent or caretaker should investigate the cause of that change. It could be the result of a physical problem or an indicator of emotional trauma such as sexual abuse.

Naturally, the most significant indicators in our lists are those which cannot be easily attributed to other causes. These are often the same behaviors we will see repeated in several of the lists given, more or less regardless of age category. For instance, in the area of sexualized behavior, when a child is discovered in sexual play which involves explicit sexual acts about which the child should have no knowledge, such behavior should not be ignored as being normal sexual experimentation.

A child may portray sexual intercourse using dolls or attempt to insert objects into another child's vagina or anus. Or parents may report that their three- or four-year-old child has attempted to initiate oral-genital sexual activity with another child. Unfortunately, in many such instances parents attempt to convince themselves or others that such behaviors are normal sex play, or that the child was imitating behavior that he or she had observed on the adult television station or in a movie. However, such is seldom the case and an effort should always be made to determine the source of the child's knowledge.

In such instances, it is important to establish whether the child learned these behaviors from another child or from an adult. The child displaying the behavior may very well have learned those activities from another child who may have in turn been sexually victimized by an adult. In some cases, we have had to interview what seemed like entire neighborhoods of children to determine the source of the sexual behavior initially observed.

Those persons concerned about indicators of sexual abuse should also keep in mind that children are sexual beings and will display some sexual activity even at a very early age. It is when a child becomes preoccupied with such activities that a parent or other concerned adult should begin to investigate the child's behavior. Children showing sexual curiosity in regard to themselves or other children close to their age need not be a cause for suspicion. On the other hand, those who compulsively masturbate at an early age or become involved in sophisticated sexual play should be.

I am reminded of several cases in which mothers reported compulsive masturbation by their three- or four-year-old daughters. These activities included the children manually manipulating themselves as well as using toys and other objects to rub against. It did not seem to matter to these children who saw them or where they were, even when they were told their actions were unacceptable.

In such instances, it is usually a simple matter to calmly question the child about her behavior and its source. In several of these cases, it was learned that the children had indeed been sexually molested, some by adults and some by older children. In others, there was no indication that any sexual abuse had taken place. But in every such case, investigation of the behavior is warranted.

There are several areas of behavior besides sexual preoccupation which are important indicators of sexual abuse among young children. Youngsters who develop sudden fears of persons or places should be questioned calmly and matter-of-factly about those fears. Consistent sleep disorders are indicative of traumas significant enough to cause disturbance in the child's subconscious mind and should not be overlooked.

Sudden changes in personality can also be important clues. When a normally secure and outgoing child refuses to be separated from a parent, even for a few moments, something is wrong. Such separation anxiety is only one personality change that might signal an emotional upset.

It is of the utmost importance that parents learn to communicate with their children in regard to these indicators. We have found that younger children are often willing to talk about what is bothering them if they are approached properly. However, as children become older it seems more difficult for them to reveal the secret of abuse because of the guilt and responsibility they feel. For this reason, it is even more important that parents be sensitive to these indicators during a child's early years. If parents or caretakers can set aside their own fears and discomfort and talk calmly and casually, most young children will readily reveal any abuse that has taken place. It is when the child senses fear or emotional instability that she might refuse to reveal the source of discomfort.

If parents are not comfortable talking to their children about such subjects but suspect some abuse may have taken place, they should be honest with themselves and seek professional help. Most child protective service agencies have people trained in effective and non-threatening interviewing techniques, and children can be interviewed in most cases without additional trauma. The worst thing a parent can do is to ignore indicators of sexual abuse in the hope that nothing really happened to the child and the suspect behavior will soon disappear of its own accord.

Behavioral Indicators in Latency-Age Children: The next category we will consider includes those behavioral indicators of sexual abuse often seen in children of latency age—that is, those children between six years of age and adolescence. This category includes the greatest number of behavioral indicators seen in any of the four age divisions. The reason for this is not completely clear, but may have something to do with the fact that statistically, most sexual abuse begins during this age period.

It is especially important that we pay close attention to the behavioral indicators listed for this age division. This is because of all the children included in these various divisions, those in the latency age range are perhaps the least likely to report their abuse. Younger children are often very open when approached properly as they have not learned to be cautious in what they say. Teenagers are likely to report because of family conflicts caused by the jealous, restrictive molester. But a child in the latency stage is old enough to be socially threatened and emotionally manipulated. At the same time, she seldom reaches the point of total desperation needed to overcome her fear of what would happen if she reported the abuse. Her feeling of responsibility to the family and her lack of resources and alternatives because of her age compound her helplessness. These victims often choose to suffer stoically, and frequently they will even deny having been sexually abused when asked directly. It is this unique set of problems that should encourage parents and professionals to be especially sensitive to the list of behavioral indicators which follows.

Behavioral Indicators of Sexual Abuse in Latency-Age Children

1. Being uncomfortable around someone previously trusted
2. Specific knowledge of sexual facts and terminology beyond developmental age
3. Sexualized behavior (excessive masturbation, sexual acting out with other children on a regular basis, seductive toward peers and adults, etc.)
4. Wearing multiple layers of clothing, especially to bed
5. Parentified behavior (pseudo-mature, acts like a small parent)
6. Fear of being alone with men or boys
7. Fear of restrooms, showers, or baths
8. Constant, unexplained anxiety, tension, or fear
9. Frequent tardiness or absence from school, especially if male caretaker writes excuses
10. Attempts to make herself ugly or undesirable (such as poor personal hygiene)

11. Eating disorders (obesity, bulimia, anorexia)
12. Self-conscious behavior, especially regarding body
13. Reluctance to go home after school
14. Abrupt personality changes
15. Child acquires toys or money with no explanation
16. Wetting of bed or clothing after being "broken" of that problem
17. Nightmares on a regular basis or about the same person
18. Change in sleeping habits (tries to stay up late or seems constantly tired)
19. Moodiness, inappropriate crying
20. Unusual need for assurance of love
21. Regressive behavior (fantasies and/or infantile behavior)
22. Uncharacteristic aggressive or violent behavior
23. Tendency to seek out or totally avoid adults
24. Inability to relate to peers
25. Running away, especially in a child normally not a behavioral problem

Many of the behaviors just enumerated are similar to those seen in the previous age division. Abrupt personality changes reflected in moodiness, excessive crying, aggressive or violent behavior, and extreme anxiety and tension are seen in both divisions and are exhibited for the same reasons. This is also true of the fear common among victims of child sexual abuse. The same fears of certain places and people, especially previously trusted individuals, are observed in these children.

Since children in this age range are usually attending school regularly, the fears just mentioned are often seen by teachers in the form of a child who is hesitant to go home after school or appears to be afraid of a particular parent. Other behaviors that teachers in particular may observe in these children include degenerating peer relationships, a tendency to be extremely self-conscious, and tardiness or absence from school, especially when a male caretaker writes excuses for the child.

Sexualized behavior and extensive knowledge of sexual facts and terminology are important indicators of abuse in this age group as well. But added to these important factors is the appearance of seductive behavior on the part of the victim during this stage. Since these children have learned at home that the only sure way to gain attention and affection is to relate sexually, it is very common for them to behave seductively toward both peers and adults.

Such behavior may also serve the function of providing these children with a measure of control over their lives. It allows them, at least in one area, to be the aggressor rather than the passive victim. For whatever reason such behavior is adopted, it seems to be a common phenomenon among female victims in this age division and is often even carried over into the victim's adult life.

In the latency age division, one can observe other efforts made by the victim to adjust to her circumstances. These vary with the background and personality of the child. Some subconsciously seek to escape through emotional regression into earlier childhood. They may develop their own fantasy worlds or revert to infantile behaviors such as baby talk and bedwetting in an effort to return to their carefree early years. Others may need to be constantly assured of parental love because of the growth of guilt and the rapid deterioration of self-image. These behaviors are generally seen among the younger victims in this age category.

Among older victims in this same division, attempts at escaping abuse may take different forms. The wearing of multiple layers of clothing and deliberate overeating are examples of some of the more passive efforts at discouraging their molesters. Occasionally victims in this age category will take the more aggressive step of running away from home, but such measures are more often seen among adolescents.

The final indicator needing comment in this division is the development of parentified or pseudo-mature behavior in many latency-age victims. Although this particular characteristic may also be seen in the other two age divisions for children, it seems to begin most often in this category. Usually described as being precocious or grown-up, these girls may skip childhood altogether and proceed to assume adult behavior and responsibility. Such behavior may be considered cute by adults, but the loss of childhood is a terrible injustice to any child and a strong indicator of child sexual abuse.

The behaviors we have listed for this age division represent desperate efforts on the part of these children to make sense of, survive, and possibly even escape sexual abuse. Unfortunately, very few succeed in preventing further victimization, and the behaviors displayed by adolescent and adult victims are testimony to the inadequacy of their coping mechanisms.

Behavioral Indicators in Adolescent Victims: By the time a victim of sexual abuse reaches adolescence, she has often lived with her nightmare for years. Not only has she been unable to stop the abuse or deal with it emotionally; she may also be faced with an increase in abusive behavior as the molester initiates full sexual intercourse or becomes extremely possessive and jealous. These girls often respond to such hopelessness and anger through behavior which is both self-abusive and retaliatory.

Unfortunately, society seems to have very little compassion for the adolescent victim of child sexual abuse. As adults, our judgment is often clouded by our impatience with normal teenage rebellion and acting-out behavior commonly mixed with the indicators of abuse seen among these children. It is hard to separate the teenager from the victim, even for professionals who should know better.

An example of this problem can be seen in one of our cases in which a teenage girl was being molested by both her stepfather and her mother. The abuse had been going on for a number of years. Desperate for help, this girl reported in detail the abuse she had been subjected to. She had hoped that her mother and stepfather would admit what they had done and get professional help. Instead they began a systematic campaign to discredit her by digging up every petty behavioral problem she had experienced as a teenager. Also, once she was placed in a foster home, her mother and stepfather blamed her for breaking up the family and refused to communicate with her further. She was able to continue her attendance at the family church but the rest of her family attended as well and shunned her in front of everyone.

Eventually the pressure became too much for this girl who loved her parents deeply, despite what they had done. She finally withdrew her original statements regarding the abuse, denying it had ever taken place. We knew from experience and from the facts of the case that she had indeed been molested and that her initial story was true. We also knew that we could not in good conscience allow her to return home as the abuse would almost surely recur.

There followed a battle in which we had to fight both the molesters and the victim to keep this girl out of danger. Eventually, in spite of all our efforts, we lost legal control of her and she was returned to the influence of those who had abused her.

During this episode the deck had been stacked against the victim because she was a teenager. People didn't seem to wonder why a girl would accuse those she loved of such abuse when she was not even angry with them. They were quick, however, to point out that she was a teenager and had experienced a few minor behavioral problems. It was even easy for us professionals to be angry with her for giving in to the pressure of her parents and fighting those who were trying to help her. But the fact of the matter is that she was a victim, both of her abuse and of her age.

The last time I saw this girl she was emotionally confused and appeared to be on the verge of a psychotic break. She is a living example of how the adolescent victim faces a peculiar dilemma in regard to her abuse.

Following is a list of behavioral indicators often observed in adolescent victims. Please keep in mind what we have just discussed as you review it.

Behavioral Indicators of Sexual Abuse in Adolescents

1. Sexualized behavior (promiscuity, prostitution, sexual abuse of younger children, etc.)
2. Running away, especially in a child normally not a behavioral problem
3. Drug and alcohol abuse
4. Suicidal gestures or attempts
5. Self-mutilation
6. Extreme hostility toward a parent or caretaker
7. Parentified behavior (pseudo-mature, acts like a small parent)
8. Self-conscious behavior, especially regarding body
9. Wearing multiple layers of clothing, especially to bed
10. Eating disorders (usually obesity)
11. Nightmares or other sleeping problems
12. Constant fear or anxiety
13. Delinquent behavior
14. School problems (academic or behavioral)
15. Defiance or compliance to an extreme
16. Friends tend to be older

Again, many of the behaviors just enumerated are seen in latency-age victims. One of the main differences between these two categories is that adolescent victims tend to be more action-oriented in their response to sexual abuse while latency-age victims are more passive. Adolescent victims experience the same emotional trauma as younger victims, but because of their growing independence and resources, they are the ones who often act out their anger through drug and alcohol abuse, prostitution, delinquent behavior, and even suicide. However, as we have already seen, the desperate actions of adolescent victims are for the most part useless in preventing the emotional fallout that tends to haunt them throughout their adult lives.

Behavioral Indicators in Adult Victims: There are a number of different behaviors displayed by adults that might indicate an individual has been the victim of sexual abuse as a child. These indicators can be especially useful to counselors attempting to determine the causes of certain problems being experienced by their clients. Remember, adults who have been sexually victimized as children seldom volunteer that information to counselors. It's not that they are trying to be secretive, just that they usually have no idea of the relationship between their previous abuse and their present problems. However, many times they will readily relate their victimization when asked directly by a counselor.

By the time a sexual abuse victim has reached adulthood, her self-abusive behavior has usually been developed to a fine science. This has all been done subconsciously and unintentionally, to be sure, but the results are the same as if the victim had deliberately set about to destroy her adult life. Following is a list of some behaviors that may tip you off to the existence of this problem and allow you to intervene on behalf of these individuals.

Behavioral Indicators of Sexual Abuse in Adults

1. Sexual difficulties (usually regarding intimacy issues)
2. Distrust of the opposite sex
3. Inappropriate choice of partners (chooses a dependent partner she can mother or one who abuses her or her children physically or sexually)
4. Progressive breakdown of communication and eventual emotional detachment from children
5. Multiple marriages
6. Extreme dependence upon or anger toward a parent
7. Sexual promiscuity (or alternating between periods of preoccupation with or revulsion by sexual activity)
8. Drug or alcohol abuse
9. Extremely low self-esteem
10. Nightmares or flashbacks
11. Continual victimization (seemingly unable to assert or protect herself)
12. May see self-worth only in sexuality
13. Eating disorders (usually obesity)
14. Self-punishing behaviors
15. Homosexual orientation
16. Body shame (extreme self-consciousness)

It is appropriate that sexual difficulties be at the top of this list since they are perhaps the most consistent indicators of sexual victimization among adults. Frigidity is one of the most common complaints among women who were victimized as children. This problem is a logical outgrowth of the child victim's effort to escape her molestation emotionally.

Children often report mentally removing themselves from the sexual act during episodes of molestation. They may determine not to give the molester the satisfaction of any response and simply want to get it over with as quickly as possible. After years of responding in such a way to any sexual activity, it is very difficult for these victims to discard these behaviors and attitudes when they begin a relationship with someone they love. The result is that frigidity or some other intimacy issue often surfaces in the marriage.

I vividly remember a statement made by a mother in one of the Christian families with whom I counseled. When sexual adjustment problems were being discussed, she said simply, "We don't have any sexual adjustment problems because I don't let him anywhere near me." Although it was never established as a fact, I strongly suspect that this mother had been sexually abused as a child and had consequently developed an extreme distaste for sexual activities of any kind. She chose a passive husband and allowed sexual intercourse only for the purpose of having children. Unfortunately, both children were girls and both were molested by their father until they left home. One daughter has chosen to avoid all social contact with men. The other has married twice and has experienced the same sexual adjustment problems as her mother in both relationships. This daughter's children are now prime candidates for sexual abuse.

Other aspects of the sexual adjustment problems seen in these adults have already been discussed in the chapters on the effects of child sexual abuse. Most of the other indicators in this list have also been explained in some detail in those chapters. It is especially important that Christian counselors become familiar with this list of indicators. Many thousands of hours of counseling time have been wasted trying to resolve symptoms of previous sexual victimization among adults without ever having discovered the root of the problem.

Family Indicators of Sexual Abuse

The signs of sexual abuse we have been discussing to this point have been those evident in the behavior of the victim. Such behaviors are mainly useful in raising an initial suspicion of sexual abuse. As these suspicions are investigated further, certain family patterns or characteristics prove useful in identifying abusive families. These family indicators have been observed with remarkable consistency in families where child sexual abuse has been proven to exist.

The family indicators of sexual abuse in the list that follows are roughly arranged so that the more significant indicators are toward the top of the list. Many of these will not be immediately visible in an abusive family. Remember, such families usually put up a good front and also tend to be secretive. The best source of information is still the suspected victim.

Family Indicators of Child Sexual Abuse

1. Role reversal between mother and daughter
2. Extreme overprotectiveness or jealousy toward a child by a parent (parent sharply restricts a child's contact with peers and adults outside the home)
3. Inappropriate sleeping arrangements (child sleeps with a parent on a regular basis or with both parents where she is exposed to sexual activity)
4. Prolonged absence of one parent from the home (through death, divorce, etc.)
5. Mother who is often ill or is disabled
6. Extreme lack of communication between caretakers
7. Inordinate participation of father in family (father may interact very little with family members or may insist on being in charge of all family activities)
8. Extreme paternal dominance of spouse (for instance, mother is not allowed to drive or to talk to school personnel, etc.)
9. Work or activity schedules which result in a caretaker (especially male) spending large amounts of time alone with a child or children
10. Extreme favoritism shown to a child (father may spend a lot of time and attention on one daughter)
11. Severe overreaction by a parent to any sex education offered a child
12. Caretaker who has been sexually abused as a child
13. Geographic isolation of family
14. Overcrowding in a home
15. Family has no social or personal support systems
16. Alcohol or drug abuse within a family

Most of these indicators will be recognized from chapter 3 on the causes of child sexual abuse. This list serves mainly to make these factors more accessible for quick review.

You will notice that social isolation is a common characteristic of abusive families. This often means that schools or other agencies having contact with the victim may know very little about the family other than what they hear from the victim. This is where pastors, Sunday school teachers, and Christian counselors have a distinct advantage. It is not uncommon for the mother and children in an incestuous family to be involved in a church while the molester either maintains his own isolation or is a nominal Christian or churchgoer who seldom gets involved in mainstream church activities. The mother may seek counseling help from the church when faced with the inevitable family problems while she might never seek such help from secular sources.

Accompanying this unique opportunity for the Christian counselor is a sobering responsibility to the children in these homes. We must resist the temptation to ignore indicators of child sexual abuse because a family appears to be a decent Christian family. The notion that Christian families might somehow be immune to this particular aspect of Satan's plan is a sign of spiritual naiveté.

Physical Indicators of Sexual Abuse

Strangely enough in our body-oriented society, the indicators of child sexual abuse which seem to be most often overlooked are the physical indicators. The reason for this is unclear, but the fact is that most discussion and training on recognizing child sexual abuse center on behavioral and family indicators. Perhaps this is because very few people consider themselves to be qualified in medical matters while many are confident of their knowledge of human behavior. Or it may be that the nature of these indicators makes it unlikely that they will ever be observed by anyone outside the family.

Whatever the reason, it should be understood that physical indicators can and should play an important role in the detection of child sexual abuse. They represent some of the most conclusive evidence of abuse available. The physical indicators enumerated in the following list are those most likely to be noticed by parents, caretakers, and teachers.

Physical Indicators of Sexual Abuse

1. Pain or itching in the genital area
2. Difficulty in walking or sitting
3. Vaginal discharge
4. Bruises or bleeding of external genitalia, vaginal, or anal regions

5. Venereal disease, especially in young children
6. Swollen or red cervix, vulva, or perineum
7. Pregnancy when a child refuses to reveal any information about the father or there is a complete denial of pregnancy by the child or her parents
8. Torn, stained, or bloody underclothing
9. Unusual and offensive odors

It is amazing how many of the obvious indicators just listed are overlooked by adults having regular contact with these children. One teacher in a local school reported having had a young girl in her fifth grade class several years ago who had a continual problem with vaginal discharge. It was so severe that eventually they had to refinish the girl's desk seat. Yet this young girl was never asked the reason for the discharge and her mother was apparently never contacted about the problem.

I have also seen several cases where daughters had purposely left semen- or blood-stained sheets and underpants in plain sight as clues to their mothers. Yet I am not aware of a single case in which a mother got the hint. Unusual or offensive odors are also often overlooked as indicators of sexual abuse. These may occur when a child is molested before school on a regular basis and does not have time to clean up before she leaves.

The other indicators included in our list are pretty much self-explanatory. However, I would issue one caution in regard to these indicators which are mostly medical in nature. It is important to remember that the best source of information on what caused the bruises, pain, swelling, and other medical problems is the child herself. Most doctors will be the first to admit they have had no specialized training in the medical detection of child sexual abuse. Only recently have any medical schools even offered such training. Also, doctors are just as uncomfortable as anyone else in confronting the issue of child sexual abuse.

The best way to get at the truth is to ask the child about what caused the problem, remembering to approach the subject casually, calmly, and privately. If you are fortunate enough to have a specially trained medical team available to you, by all means, take advantage of that resource. But remember, the victim is the ultimate authority.

Listening between the Lines

Even though a child victim of sexual abuse will often discuss her victimization when approached properly, it is important to keep in mind that these children seldom report their abuse directly, especially to those who may be hurt by such a report. Children are especially sensitive to the feelings of those they love. In addition, child victims are usually suffering from guilt and fear. Consequently, adults need to be able to listen between the lines when children are talking.

Most children who are victims of sexual abuse will drop verbal hints about what has happened and will then wait for a response. They may make a passing statement about a parent or other adult they do not like to be around. Or they may relate the problem of a friend who has been approached sexually by an adult. Seldom will any of these victims pursue the matter further if the adult they are talking to seems uninterested or emotionally threatened.

Compounding this problem is the fact that adults do not want to admit to themselves that such things actually happen. Parents are especially hesitant to believe that one or more of their own children may have been victims of sexual abuse. But we as concerned adults must overcome their investment in ignorance and be sensitive to what our children are saying, not only directly, but through their behavior and hidden messages.

Should we be hesitant to develop such a sensitivity to the children around us, perhaps a review of our chapters on the effects of child sexual abuse would be in order. Those of us who are willing to hear what is really being said by our children can only hope that the message conveyed will not include a report of sexual abuse. However, if it should, we must be prepared to deal with this problem immediately and effectively. What we as adults do in response to such a report can literally mean the difference between devastation and health in the emotional lives of these children.

CHAPTER NINE

Between a Rock and a Hard Place

Melanie was four years old when her mother became concerned about some changes in her behavior. This usually cheerful and talkative child suddenly became sullen and withdrawn. When she did speak she would whine and use baby talk. She also began sucking her thumb, which she had not done for over two years.

Melanie's mother could not imagine what could be causing such a regression in her behavior. One day she wisely took her daughter aside and had a casual, lengthy talk with her. Melanie was at first hesitant to talk about what was bothering her. However, as she became more relaxed and saw that her mother was reacting calmly to what she was saying, Melanie finally related that her father had sexually molested her on several of her weekend visits with him. She had slept in his bed and he had fondled her, and he also had her touch him.

Even though Melanie's mother was horrified by what she heard, she managed to remain calm, told Melanie she believed her and arranged for her to be interviewed by someone with experience in such matters. The resulting interviews, in which sexually detailed dolls were used, confirmed the suspicion of sexual abuse.

Melanie's father denied having abused her. The criminal case was never prosecuted because Melanie's age and emotional state would have made her a poor witness. However, Melanie did get the protection she needed. And because she was able to talk to her mother and others about the problem, she is doing well emotionally. She was fortunate to have a mother who responded correctly to her report of sexual abuse. The outlook for her future is bright and there is a good chance that emotional damage will be minimal in her case.

Michelle, who is now eight, was not so fortunate. Not long after her mother had married for the second time, her new stepfather, Jim, had begun to sexually molest her. After several months of molestation, Michelle's mother questioned her about her increasingly hostile and violent behavior. Michelle finally reported what Jim had been doing. Her mother was speechless. But she finally regained her composure and told Michelle she would talk to her later about it. She approached Jim who vehemently denied everything, saying that Michelle had to be crazy to say such a thing.

Michelle's mother had a lot at stake in this matter. She was now middle-aged without any skills or means of support other than Jim. She also felt she was not attractive enough to find another husband if this marriage should fail. Also, Jim seemed so sincere, so insistent and intense in his denials. Without even talking to Michelle again, her mother agreed, at Jim's suggestion, to commit Michelle to a private mental institution. The yearly fee of twenty thousand dollars was no problem for Jim, who was a very successful businessman.

Michelle was confined to that facility for one year before returning home. Predictably, the molestation resumed almost immediately. This time Michelle, having learned her lesson, was not about to tell her mother of the abuse. It was not until this year that a teacher became concerned about her deteriorating performance in school and the occasional sexual themes in her artwork. Michelle's teacher reported her suspicions to the appropriate authorities and the resulting investigation revealed the ongoing sexual abuse. Her mother was eventually forced to believe Michelle when confronted with details she had given about Jim and his sexual preferences.

Unfortunately, the emotional damage done to Michelle by her abuse and her mother's attitude had been extensive. Despite counseling, she continues to display signs of permanent emotional damage. The road ahead for her appears to be rough.

How parents respond when a child reports sexual abuse is *very important* in determining the amount of emotional damage sustained by the victim. An incorrect response can compound the emotional damage already done, expose the child to further abuse, and destroy communication between parent and child. On the other hand, by being supportive and sensitive to the victim, parents can often arrest emotional damage and start the child on the road to recovery.

It is also important for pastors and other counselors to be aware of the best way to respond to children who reveal that they have been sexually abused. In addition to their important part in the initial support of the victim, it often becomes necessary for such individuals to assume the temporary role of the child's advocate and to help cushion the blow to the family when the subject of abuse is confronted. It is at this point that the most support is needed by both victim and family.

Prayer Changes Things

Our first response as Christians to this or any other problem in our lives should be to seek God's help. It is my personal belief that prayer is an effective weapon against the damage that sexual abuse causes. We serve a supernatural and miraculous God who is very much concerned with the family in general and children in particular. Admittedly, some of my learned colleagues may scoff at the notion of using prayer as an avenue of help in such cases. Nevertheless, such is God's plan and desire. In his letter to the Corinthian church, Paul made it clear that while God's ways seem to be foolishness to the world, they are actually powerful and wise. "For the foolishness of God is wiser than men, and the weakness of God is stronger than men" (1 Cor. 1:25).

Parents faced with the terrible specter of child sexual abuse need to pray not only for the healing of their children, but for wisdom in how to respond to the problem. In James 1:5 Christians are admonished to pray for wisdom when it is needed.

> If any of you lacks wisdom, let him ask God, who gives to all men generously and without reproaching, and it will be given him.

Nothing I can say will adequately prepare people for the shock experienced when molestation comes to light. The best thing parents can do is to cast their cares and concerns on God because he cares for them (1 Peter 5:7).

Not only will prayer provide parents with comfort and supernatural wisdom; it will also help calm them emotionally before they take those all-important initial steps in dealing with the problem. Without such calmness, even a well-meaning and conscientious parent or counselor can destroy a child's life.

Once parents have taken the problem before God and received supernatural assistance and peace, they will need to know how to respond correctly to the victims themselves. Following are lists of practical guidelines on how best to handle the victims without causing further emotional damage.

What to Do If Your Child Reports Sexual Abuse

Immediately

1. Take your child to a private place and ask the child to explain what happened in her own words. Listen carefully and remember to be calm and matter-of-fact.

2. Believe your child! Children seldom lie about sexual abuse.
3. Assure your child that what happened is not her fault, and that you are glad she told you.
4. Tell your child you are sorry she was hurt and scared and that you will protect her from further abuse.
5. Call an agency that has expertise in the field of sexual abuse. Most areas have a child protective service agency. Check with local law enforcement agencies for information.
6. If what your child says causes you to suspect that sexual penetration or physical injury has occurred, seek medical attention for your child immediately and inform the doctor of your suspicions.
7. Take whatever steps are necessary to protect your child from further abuse. In the case of incest, see that the molester, not the victim, leaves the home.

Assisting Your Child Following the Initial Report

1. Continue to support your child. Never question the child about why she did not tell sooner or make any statements that might imply guilt.
2. Reassure your child that what happened was not her fault and does not make her a bad person.
3. Do not encourage your child to forget about the molestation.
4. Allow your child to talk about what happened any time she desires to do so. When you respond, remember to be calm and matter-of-fact.
5. Do not be surprised or upset by expressions of anger or love toward the molester. Your child may still love the molester even though she is very angry about what that person did.
6. Calmly instruct your child in what to do should such a situation arise again.
7. Don't change the routine of the home or relax rules or responsibilities for the victim.
8. Protect your child's privacy by not telling too many people about what happened.
9. If your child must be questioned, insist that agencies combine interviews or tape an interview for review by others who must know the facts.
10. For your own sake, talk to a pastor, counselor, or trusted friend about the feelings you are experiencing as a result of what happened, but not in front of your children.

The guidelines just given are most important in safeguarding the emotional health of the victim. You may see fit to modify them to meet your particular circumstances. However, please be sure to read the remainder of this chapter first in order to understand some of the reasons behind the recommendations.

Insult to Injury

In situations where a child is molested by someone outside the family, the response of the parents is much less likely to harm a child than is the case with incestuous abuse. When the molester is a stranger, the parents of the victim will usually be very supportive of the child. The enemy is clearly identified, and while anger and hatred are factors, they are generally directed toward the molester. While parents may express some anger toward the child for being in the wrong place at the wrong time, their stance is generally supportive of the victim. Consequently, emotional harm in such cases is likely to be minimal, unless violence or other exceptional factors were involved.

This is rarely the case when an incestuous relationship is reported. When incest is uncovered, the non-offending parent (usually the mother) who learns of the abuse often experiences a series of extreme emotional reactions that may cause her to lose sight of the victim's need for support and comfort. In her own pain and confusion, she may strike out at the victim and greatly compound the damage already done.

When a mother learns that her partner has been sexually abusing her child, she usually enters a state of emotional shock. Confusion reigns as she attempts to sort out what happened. She wants to believe the child but finds it hard to disregard the loud, insistent denials of her partner. At the same time, even considering the possibility that her husband might have done such a terrible thing fills her with disgust and anger.

If she believes her child, she is flooded with feelings of guilt for not protecting the child and for what she may perceive as her failure to meet her husband's sexual needs. She feels betrayed—both by her husband, who chose a child over her as a sexual partner, and by her daughter, who had waited so long to reveal the molestation. On top of all this, she is angry for being forced to choose between two people she loves.

All of these conflicting and explosive feelings can understandably cause the non-offending parent to do and say things that might result in further damage to the child victim. But it is crucial that she overcome her inclination to take out her anger and frustration on the victim. It is easy for a mother to be so overwhelmed with anger toward the abuser that she lashes out at her child for not telling sooner or for leading him on. I have seen too many mothers destroy their own children because the molester was either unavailable or too threatening to confront. Such misguided actions foster a hatred in the heart of the victim, one that may never be resolved.

On the other side of the coin, these mothers have a rare opportunity to develop with their children one of the strongest of all human relationships, that born out of mutual support in adversity. Mothers who support their daughters during the crisis of reported incest often find that their daughters support them in return. Some of the most beautiful mother-daughter relationships I have ever seen have come out of the ash heap of incest.

Double Jeopardy

The next important task to undertake after the initial report of child sexual abuse is the protection of the child from further molestation. Most people respond to such a statement with comments like, "Of course I would protect my child. Wouldn't any parent?" Indeed, a high percentage of parents do take action to protect their children when the molester is a stranger. But incest is a different matter altogether, and many factors complicate the question of protection.

In a recent study conducted by a sexual assault center in the state of Washington, some interesting tendencies were observed among the parents of sexual abuse victims. It was learned in this study that when children who had been molested by strangers reported the molestation to their parents, 85 percent of those parents took immediate action to protect their children from further abuse. On the other hand, among families in which a child had reported incestuous abuse directly to a parent, only 60 percent of those parents took immediate action to protect their children.[16]

These figures are especially disturbing in light of the fact that incest victims are much more likely to be re-molested than are children who have been sexually abused by strangers. In fact, the same study also showed that more than 90 percent of the incest victims surveyed had been subjected to molestation on more than one occasion. This was true in only 27 percent of the cases of sexual abuse outside the family.

Why is it so hard for the non-offending parent in an incest family to take actions necessary for the protection of her child? Remember that in order to take such actions, the mother must first admit that the abuse did in fact take place. And in making such an admission, she must also concede the fact that her husband has chosen a young girl in preference to her as a sexual partner. In addition to these brutal realities, she must also face fears of family disintegration, financial hardships, loneliness, and social rejection, to mention only a few.

The molester, when confronted with the accusation of sexual abuse, usually responds in one of two ways. Either he vehemently and stubbornly denies the abuse, or he quickly admits his guilt and repents with tears and promises. Most refuse to admit their guilt and prove to be extremely effective in recruiting their mates as allies, especially since the non-offending parent has a lot to lose by believing the victim. I've lost count of how many times we've begged mothers to take protective measures for their children even if they won't admit to believing the child's story. Unfortunately, few take our advice—but most eventually wish they had.

Even when a molester readily admits guilt, he is often able to convince his partner that he is truly sorry for what he has done and that it will never happen again. But the promises of a molester are empty, containing nothing but false hope. And the mother who believes them is consenting to the continued abuse of her child. That is not to say that a molester doesn't mean what he says. He often does. In fact, many genuinely convince themselves after each sexual contact that they will never do it again. Unfortunately, their compulsion is usually stronger than their good intentions.

If the non-offending parent does believe the report of her child, she is faced with some hard choices. First of all, she can choose to ignore the problem and hope that it goes away. We have already pointed out the foolishness of such a decision. She may choose to report the abuse to the appropriate authorities and let the established procedures run their course. We will deal specifically with some of the legal and moral implications of such a decision later in this chapter. Finally, she may decide to try and resolve the problem within the family rather than seeking outside help. Should the non-offending parent choose this last course of action, she may find that she has taken upon herself a difficult, if not impossible, task. The fact is that most molesters are experts at manipulation, so it is extremely difficult to work with them and protect the victim at the same time. After all, many of these individuals have managed to sexually molest children in their own homes over a period of years without being caught. If the non-offending parent expects to have any hope at all of preventing further abuse, she must be willing to take some drastic measures toward that end.

First of all, these mothers must realize that they cannot, for any reason, allow the victim or a female sibling to be alone with the molester for *any* length of time. A responsible adult should be present at all times—not just in the house or around the area, but close enough to maintain visual contact with these children. This may sound ridiculous, but it is not. Molesters, even the "nice" ones, are resourceful individuals driven by compulsive needs. Protective precautions must be extreme and consistent for the sake of the victim.

I have seen many instances in which a father molested a child while his wife was in the next room. A few I know of have even done so with their wives in the same room, and one grandfather even managed to molest his granddaughter in the back of a boat while her parents were in the front. It is important that siblings also be protected, as a molester will often molest another child in the family when deprived of his initial victim.

There are further precautions that will need to be taken if the non-offending parent decides to handle this problem on her own. Since abusive acts often take place in a child's room during the night, it will be necessary to insure the privacy of each child through the use of locks or latches. Simple hook or bolt latches are sufficient for this purpose, but children must be encouraged to use them consistently. Privacy in general seems often to be a problem in incestuous families and is an area that needs special attention. Aside from insuring privacy at night, the non-offending parent should also see that her children are allowed privacy while using the bathroom. Bathrooms are common settings for the initiation of sexual abuse "routines."

Here are two final precautions for the mother who insists on going it alone. First, if the molester admits his guilt and agrees to get counseling, remember that very few counselors have any experience in this field. If your partner happens to get an untrained counselor, he will soon have that counselor convinced that he is cured or that he had simply made a few mistakes. An adept molester can usually manage to be released from counseling by the end of the second or third session. Most legitimate counseling programs for molesters include intensive individual and group therapy which lasts from nine months to three years.

The second precaution is very important to the victim and to your family as a whole. If you decide you cannot protect the victim adequately, or that family problems require a separation of the molester and the victim, *please* insist that the molester leave rather than the victim. I realize that it may be much simpler and less threatening to have the victim leave the home in such a case, but it is extremely important that she be allowed to remain.

First, the victim usually perceives her removal from the home as punishment. It identifies her as the problem within the family and reinforces her false feelings of guilt. Second, it has been our experience that such arrangements usually end in the alienation of mother and daughter. Once the victim is out of the home, it is much easier for the molester to get the non-offending parent back on his side. Every effort should be made to preserve the bond between mother and victim. It is the most important building block in the reconstruction of the family.

Law, Justice, and Mercy

When considering what course of action to take after the discovery of sexual abuse, it is helpful not only to be aware of the human aspects of the problem but also the legal issues involved. As you might imagine, consideration of the legal issues surrounding child sexual abuse is greatly complicated by the fact that every state has its own laws relating to this subject. In addition, each county or legal jurisdiction has its own policies in regard to enforcement, and each judge has his or her own interpretation of the existing laws. The best we can do in this book is give you some general guidelines on the subject and refer you to other more specific sources of information.

Sexual relations between adults and children are illegal in every state. However, the laws that prohibit such activity do so under a multitude of titles, including "incest," "sexual misconduct," "sexual abuse of minors," and "indecency with a child," just to name a few. Incest is generally defined *legally* as sexual intercourse between blood relatives, but since the cases we define as incest often do not involve actual intercourse or may be initiated by molesters not related to the victims, such cases must be dealt with under different legal categories. Readers interested in specific information on child sexual abuse laws in a particular state or jurisdiction should contact their local district attorney's office.

The question of criminal penalty for acts of child sexual abuse is also extremely complicated and is constantly changing due to the increased attention this subject is receiving. In general, the penalties for such crimes depend on the extent of the sexual activity in question, the age of the child, and the amount of force or coercion used. In theory, the punishment for sexually abusing a child can be quite severe, with several states even allowing for the death penalty under certain circumstances. But in practice, legal penalties tend to be light, especially in the case of incest. Some states even classify such crimes as misdemeanors and allow the judge to impose a fine instead of incarceration. It is quite common for individuals convicted of child sexual abuse to receive no punishment other than a period of probation, especially on their first offense.

The truth is that very few cases of child sexual abuse are ever reported to the authorities. It is estimated that less than 5 percent of all instances of child sexual abuse are reported to any agency. Of those cases that are reported, only a fraction result in an arrest and still fewer are actually prosecuted in court. Even in cases that do come to trial, the general bias toward the defendant in our legal system makes the conviction of a molester difficult at best.

While the legal system in our nation has done much to protect the rights of the accused, it has made little allowance for the problems experienced by child victims. These children are often callously treated by everyone from the investigating officer to the judge. They are forced to confront the molester and are often subjected to hours of hostile and confusing questioning in open courtrooms filled with strangers. A ten-year-old child recently spent fifteen hours testifying in a preliminary hearing regarding alleged sexual abuse in a California day care center. Before the case was even scheduled to go to trial this child had already suffered an emotional ordeal that many adults would have trouble handling.

Some progress is being made toward more humane treatment of children in our courts through the use of closed-circuit television and the video-taping of testimony. But it remains to be seen whether such measures will hold up under constitutional challenge. If we ever hope to effectively combat the threat of child sexual abuse, we must make every effort to see that the legal system in our nation responds to the needs of these children.

Many people ask why we are so anxious to uncover sexual abuse if children are mistreated and traumatized when it does come to light. This question seems to have its roots in a common misconception often voiced by media commentators when discussing child sexual abuse. These commentators regularly state with authority that what happens to a child after the discovery of sexual abuse often is more damaging to that child than the abuse itself. This is utter nonsense!

As serious as it may be, the emotional upset and family disruption that result from the discovery of sexual abuse cannot begin to compare to the crippling emotional destruction suffered by the victim when sexual abuse is allowed to continue. Ignoring sexual abuse because its discovery will initially traumatize the child and her family is like deciding not to remove an operable cancer because the procedure will be painful for the patient. The future of the child must be our primary consideration, for it is in the victim's future that the full extent of the damage will be seen.

I am well aware of the dilemma facing the reader who knows of or suspects child sexual abuse. I have often had to stand helplessly by and watch people wrestle with problems for which there are no perfect solutions. Not long ago I received a call from a desperate mother. She had learned some time back during a conversation with her seven-year-old son that his stepfather had molested him on several occasions. This mother had believed and supported her son in spite of the stepfather's emphatic denials. Unfortunately, she had chosen to leave the home and divorce her husband without reporting the abuse in order to spare her son the added trauma of an investigation and trial. All she wanted from us was information on treatment. It seems her son had developed some emotional problems as the result of his victimization. While informing this mother of the available treatment resources, I learned from her that the molester still lived in our area. He was a prominent businessman and community leader who was being considered by his party as a candidate for state office. She had also found out through a private investigator that this individual had at one time been accused of a similar incident of sexual abuse in another area. As much as I tried, I could not convince her to allow her son to be interviewed or to provide me with the information I needed to complete an investigation.

While I appreciated the concern of this mother for her son's welfare, I also know that child molesters rarely stop molesting simply because they lose access to one victim. The chances are that this individual will seek out another family with young boys and continue his pattern of abuse. And even if he confines his actions to children within that family unit, those children could have been spared victimization if the mother of the previous victim had properly reported her son's molestation. If the molester happens to be the type who abuses children outside of the home as well, the potential for harm is staggering. I have heard such molesters boast of having sexually abused hundreds of children in a period of a few months.

I cannot pretend to be the social conscience for all parents who learn that their child has been sexually abused. I cannot even promise that I would take my own advice if I were to learn that a child of mine had been molested. But I can relate facts for your consideration. And it is a fact that there are thousands of children being molested in this nation each year who would not have been if the parents of previous victims had reported the abuse of their children.

If you are in such a moral dilemma regarding whether to report sexual abuse, please at least take the time to call your local child protective service agency and talk to someone about your problem. You do not have to give your name or any other information you do not wish to. They can provide you with valuable information on the laws and procedures that apply to your particular circumstances. For those of you who are unsure of which local agency to contact, I have included in Appendix A a list of state information centers you can call for assistance. You owe it to yourself and your child to obtain as much information as possible before making such an important decision.

CHAPTER TEN

Where Do We Go from Here?

Now that we have discussed how to recognize child sexual abuse and what to do immediately upon its discovery, we need to consider the subject of treatment. In some cases of sexual abuse, formal treatment may not even be necessary and the damage done to the victim can be remedied by an understanding and supportive parent. In most cases, however, formal counseling is helpful and often is absolutely necessary to the well-being of both victim and family.

This chapter will deal mainly with the treatment of sexual abuse within the family. The treatment principles discussed may be applicable to any child in need of treatment because of sexual abuse, whether she is a victim of incest or sexual abuse by a stranger. However, in cases of sexual abuse outside the family, the treatment of the victim's family is usually not necessary and treatment of the molester becomes the concern of society.

For all individuals affected by the problem of incest, an understanding of the dynamics of child sexual abuse and the realization that they are not alone in their problem are in themselves important parts of the treatment process. But knowledge alone is rarely adequate to resolve the family and emotional problems that result from incest. Thus, it is often necessary to seek outside help when sexual abuse is discovered.

It may be helpful at this point to enumerate some of the factors that seem to bear on the amount of damage suffered by the victim. These factors are those commonly seen and reported by professionals working in this field and are based on professional observations made in thousands of cases of sexual abuse. However, we should again be reminded that children are individuals and will often respond differently to similar situations. With this in mind, let us consider the following general list of damage factors.

Damage Factors in Child Sexual Abuse

1. **The relationship of the molester to the victim:** The more closely related or highly trusted the molester, the more damage done to the child.
2. **The use of force or violence:** The more force or violence, the greater the damage, especially if serious physical injuries result.
3. **The degree of non-violent coercion:** The greater the amount of fear and guilt used in controlling the victim, the more serious the damage.
4. **The extent of abuse:** Intercourse is more emotionally harmful than genital exposure or other non-contact forms of abuse. However, extensive and long-term fondling has been found in some instances to rival the damage caused by intercourse.
5. **The duration of abuse:** Sexual abuse which takes place over a long period of time tends to be more harmful than that of short duration.
6. **The number and frequency of incidents:** The more numerous and frequent the incidents, the greater the emotional damage.
7. **The age and developmental status of the victim:** Generally, the older the victim and the more aware she is of the nature of what occurred, the more serious the emotional harm done.
8. **The reactions of significant adults to the report of abuse:** The less emotional support the victim receives from her family members and the community, the greater the degree of damage.

This list is by no means all-inclusive and should only be one of the considerations in evaluating the treatment needs of a child victim. The factors given are subjective and open to interpretation. Each individual will have to weigh their importance, taking into consideration the personality of the child and other significant factors that cannot be categorized. However, as a general guideline, in any case where a child is subjected to a high degree of harm as defined in even one of these categories, counseling is strongly suggested.

It is my professional opinion that *all* incest cases as we have defined them require professional intervention. Conversely, if a child is subjected to one incident of genital exposure by a stranger and is appropriately supported by her parents, counseling will likely not be necessary. For the reader who is not sure of which course to take, I suggest that it is better to err on the side of caution and seek help—but be sure it's qualified help.

Treatment Resources

There are many different types of professional counseling help available to individuals and families throughout the nation. Some are more appropriate than others in dealing with the problem of child sexual abuse. The classic form of Freudian psychoanalysis is often the first treatment model people think of when professional counseling is mentioned. The therapist's couch and bearded analyst are images burned deeply into the American consciousness. However, for quite some time now the trend in professional circles has been away from such traditional forms of therapy and toward a broad and growing field of new treatment methods. A list of such recently developed methods might include Gestalt Therapy, Reality Therapy, Transactional Analysis, Encounter Therapy, Biofeedback, and Assertiveness Training, to name just a few. Some of these methods are used primarily in individual therapy, while others may be employed in group therapy—and some are even applicable to both.

In regard to choosing between individual and group therapy, it is my opinion that individual therapy is most useful in the treatment of children who have been sexually abused by strangers and as a supplemental therapy in treating members of incest families. As far as I am concerned, the treatment of choice in cases of incest should be group counseling, especially when such groups are specifically designed to deal with the problem of incest. When a child is molested outside the family, a qualified counselor can usually deal with the problem on a one-to-one basis. However, if the abuse is within the family, treatment becomes extremely complicated and is best handled through a specialized treatment program stressing group therapy.

The incest treatment programs which seem to have the most success usually employ a model of group counseling supplemented by specialized individual counseling. These programs provide treatment groups for victims, non-offending caretakers, molesters, and adults who were molested as children. In all good sexual abuse treatment programs, counselors are specifically trained in the dynamics of child sexual abuse. Without such training, they are ill-equipped to handle the unique problems faced by these families.

Treatment groups have the advantage of providing both peer pressure and peer support during the treatment process. As a result of their own experiences, group members who are further advanced in therapy can often recognize the games played by newcomers. They also provide emotional support where needed and act as examples of what proper treatment can accomplish. Another benefit of groups is that they provide a means of reducing the client's feelings of isolation.

Unfortunately, there are few Christian resources available for the treatment of sexual abuse victims and their families. It is hoped that this book will help remedy that situation and that, through education and organization, the church will soon be able to offer more services to these families from a Christian perspective. Meanwhile, it may be necessary to use the programs available in the public sector. I believe it is entirely possible for the Christian to benefit from such programs if proper precautions are taken and the Christian is careful also to apply biblical principles during the treatment process. The only alternatives are to ignore the need for treatment or to seek treatment from uninformed counselors. Both of these hold the potential for unthinkable disaster.

Fortunately, one of the best secular incest treatment programs presently in operation is also one of the most available. Parents United, as this program is commonly referred to, currently has more than 130 chapters throughout the United States. Headquartered in San Jose, California, this program has been functioning since the early 1970s and is one of the most recognized incest treatment programs in the nation. The Child Sexual Abuse Treatment Programs started throughout the country by this organization follow the basic model of group and individual treatment just discussed.

As one would expect with any large organization, treatment effectiveness in the different chapters of Parents United varies according to staffing, experience, and public support. Information about the Parents United chapter nearest you and instructions on how to contact other sexual abuse treatment programs in your area are included in Appendix B.

For those who decide to obtain individual counseling on their own, the nearest sexual abuse treatment program can probably give you a list of qualified therapists. Many of the larger sexual abuse treatment programs do not charge for their services as private counselors almost always do, but many states now have victim compensation funds available to help with counseling expenses. Information on financial assistance for victims and their families can usually be obtained from local law enforcement agencies or district attorneys.

In California, victim compensation funds are even available to adults who were molested as children. These funds cover the cost of counseling needed by other family members as well as the victim herself. They also pay for transportation expenses and loss of wages and do not require a criminal conviction for eligibility. While the requirements and benefits of victim compensation funds vary from state to state, it is well worth your while to investigate the matter further.

If you are tempted to initiate a self-treatment program in lieu of the resources just discussed, you should give a great deal of prayerful consideration to such a decision. It is possible to gain some therapeutic benefit from the reading of this book and the personal application of pertinent Scriptures. But a very important part of therapy for the victim of sexual abuse is the discussion of her feelings with another individual or group. The feedback and emotional support provided under such circumstances can greatly enhance the healing process. Should you decide in spite of what has been said to attempt self-treatment, carefully read this entire book. I also recommend a book entitled *A House Divided* by Katherine Edwards, published by Zondervan Books. Her book is especially helpful for an adult who was molested as a child. But my first recommendation is to get specialized professional help.

Treatment Priorities

With treatment resources and trained personnel so limited, it is necessary to develop some priorities on what segments of treatment are most important to the incest family. Such considerations have to do not only with personnel and finances, but also with family dynamics. Often when working with a sexually abusive family, it becomes clear that the family unit cannot be maintained intact, at least for the time being. Choices must be made on which family members and relationships have treatment priority.

The Victim: The philosophy of most reputable incest treatment programs is that the victim is the number one treatment priority in the incest family. She is, after all, the one who has suffered the most harm and will therefore require the greatest amount of help if she is to lead anything resembling a normal life.

There are several important factors to keep in mind while treating the victim in an incest family. Some of these also apply to children who have been victims of other forms of sexual abuse and even to adults who were molested as children. If these factors are not addressed by the victim during treatment, the therapist should bring them up for discussion since it is very important that they be resolved.

The first issue that needs to be considered in treating sexual abuse victims is the establishment of blame. The fact that most of these victims blame themselves for what happened is a major barrier to effective treatment. Until the molester is established as the guilty party, treatment progress will be minimal. It will be necessary for everyone involved in the treatment process to repeatedly reinforce the fact that the victim is not to blame for what happened to her and that the abuser, being the adult, was responsible for molesting a child. Counselors who do not find themselves growing weary of making such a statement during treatment are probably not doing it enough. Remember, the false guilt caused by years of repetitive conditioning may take years of repetitive conditioning to erase.

The next most important consideration in treating the incest victim is the establishment of the mother-daughter bond. This task must be accomplished as quickly as possible after the discovery of abuse. By encouraging the mother to believe and support her daughter, the treatment program not only provides vital emotional support to the daughter, but to the mother as well. If such a relationship is not developed immediately, the victim's mother will often end up taking the molester's side, depriving the victim of any parental support during her ordeal. The best way to accomplish bonding is to bring mother and daughter together immediately after the abuse is discovered. When face to face with her daughter, the mother usually finds it easier to believe the daughter's report and to empathize with what she must have gone through. If the mother is still hesitant to believe the victim's story, some programs allow her to listen to her daughter's taped statement. It is hard not to believe these children when you hear their description of what happened to them.

If the mother-daughter bond can be established, a very important step has been taken in the healing of both the victim and her family. If not, treatment will be an uphill battle and the chances of saving the family intact will be greatly reduced. This is one of the main reasons that experts in this field recommend the molester, not the victim, leave the home.

Another thing counselors should know is that incest victims often display ambivalent feelings toward both the molester and the non-offending parent. By this I mean that a victim may express hatred for her molester on one occasion and a short time later be crying because she misses him. Likewise, she may at times display extreme anger toward her mother, to whom she is usually very close.

Some therapists learn about such conflicting feelings the hard way when they try to remove the victim's guilt by making frequent derogatory remarks about the molester. They may be surprised when the victim defends her molester and becomes angry with the counselor. It should be remembered that the victim can hate the abusive aspects of her relationship with the molester and still love him very much. After all, in many of these families the only attention and support the victim has received has come from the molester. The fact that he perverted their relationship usually does not erase the positive aspects of that relationship in the victim's mind.

In regard to her ambivalent feelings toward her mother, it is common for the victim to be more angry with her mother than with the molester. This is mainly due to the victim's belief that her mother failed to stop the abuse when she could have. I have often heard victims chastise their mothers with statements like, "He was sick, but you didn't have any excuse. You should have protected me." These feelings of anger are often present even when a strong and loving mother-daughter relationship has been established, and it is important that they be dealt with in treatment. But joint mother-daughter sessions should be attempted only after both parties have gained insight and emotional strength through separate counseling. Otherwise, the daughter may come expecting her mother to admit negligence, and her mother may not be prepared for the hostility she encounters. This issue is often one of the last to be addressed in treatment, but it is one of the most important to resolve.

Another aspect of treatment which needs to be addressed in regard to the incest victim is her confrontation with the molester. Many incest treatment plans promote the use of a face to face confrontation between victim and molester as a therapeutic tool. The problem is that many such confrontations occur without proper preparation and are accompanied by too great an expectation on the part of the victim. In such instances, the confrontation may do more harm than good.

The victim-molester confrontation can be useful in therapy but should only be attempted under certain circumstances. Generally, the victim desires such a confrontation because she hopes the molester will admit his guilt and repent of his actions. She wants to be convinced of his regret and his desire to change. Unfortunately, these sessions seldom turn out as the victim had hoped, especially if they take place in an unsupervised treatment setting and the victim is the only family member in counseling. Often a child victim or an adult who was molested as a child will choose to confront her parents in her own home. With the parents unprepared for such a situation and still maintaining their old defense mechanisms, such impromptu sessions are almost always disastrous.

The victim should be prepared for such a meeting well in advance. She first needs to gain insight into her family and the dynamics that allowed sexual abuse to develop. She also needs to be aware of her own feelings and expectations about what might happen and prepare herself emotionally for the worst. Then, if her parents react defensively or with denial, she is braced for the disappointment. At least she is able to rid herself of the terrible family secret by expressing it verbally to the principle players.

The confrontation between the victim and molester should ideally take place under the supervision of a qualified counselor in a neutral setting, but such arrangements are seldom possible because of the molester's refusal to cooperate. If this is the case, an informal confrontation initiated by the victim may prove useful if she has been properly prepared. In such an instance, the victim may find it helpful to be accompanied by a counselor or fellow victim who can lend emotional support.

Yet another treatment problem must be considered when dealing with the incest victim. It is likely that at some point during therapy both counselor and client will be faced with the victim's feelings about her loss of childhood and the betrayal of innocence caused by her victimization. The natural tendency of the concerned therapist in such a situation is to try to rescue the victim from her sense of sorrow and to focus on the promise of the future. While there is nothing wrong with encouraging the client in regard to the future, she should first be allowed to mourn her past. Grieving clears the way for future emotional growth. Unfortunately, grief is a threatening emotion to many counselors who may try to sidetrack those feelings by focusing on another issue. The victim needs permission from her counselor to grieve and emotional support while her grief is being expressed.

The final and perhaps the most important priority in treating victims of sexual abuse is forgiveness. While very few secular treatment programs concern themselves with forgiveness and some even discourage it, it is a subject that must be considered by Christians seeking God's perspective on sexual abuse. God has made it clear in his Word that forgiveness is an essential part of the Christian life. In Matthew 6:14–15, Jesus told his disciples:

> For if you forgive men their trespasses, your heavenly Father also will forgive you; but if you do not forgive men their trespasses, neither will your Father forgive your trespasses.

This is a pretty plain statment of God's viewpoint on the subject of forgiveness.

Many victims of sexual abuse are convinced that it is impossible for them to forgive their molesters or those who stood by without helping. Counselors working with this problem may feel the same way. However, I am convinced that God has not asked us to do anything that is beyond our ability with his help. I appreciate the comments made by Katherine Edwards on this subject as she wrote about her own experiences as an incest victim in her book, *A House Divided.* At one point she had argued with God about whether it was possible for her to forgive such a terrible transgression. She related that it was not until she was able to see past her stepfather's facade of anger that she began to pity him for what he really was—a lonely and miserable individual. Even then she found it difficult to forgive but asked God to change her heart if that was what he really wanted. Let me quote to you her final argument with God as she fought the idea of forgiveness.

> "Lord, how can I ever forgive him for what he did to me?"
>
> "What is the difference between what he did to you and all his other sins?"
>
> "Nothing, really, except that I was the victim." I found myself getting uncomfortable.
>
> "What particular sin of his will condemn him to hell?"
>
> "Only the sin of not accepting Jesus Christ as his personal Savior."
>
> "Not his violation of your body?"
>
> "No, not even that." My answers were less bold. The focus of my hatred was becoming blurred.
>
> "What then, is the difference between his sin and yours?"
>
> "None—except that mine has been forgiven through the blood of Christ."
>
> "If I can forgive you, why are you unable to forgive your stepfather?"
>
> "But Lord, what he did to me was so terrible!" My throat constricted with tears as I clung to the last vestiges of self.
>
> "What did your sins do to my Son?"
>
> "They nailed Him to a cross."
>
> I sat silently for a long time after that. There was no question now: I would, by choice of will, forgive.[17]

Katherine Edwards found that as she forgave, her nightmares diminished and her whole outlook on life changed. Forgiveness freed her to get on with her life. Victims who refuse to forgive find that their anger and hatred are more damaging to them than to their molesters. God realizes that Christians experience anger, unforgiveness, and even hatred. He also makes it clear that the best way to deal with such feelings is to get rid of them. In Ephesians 4:26–27, Paul tells the Christians at Ephesus,

> Be ye angry, and sin not: let not the sun go down upon your wrath: Neither give place to the devil (KJV).

I believe God wants us to face the existence of such destructive emotions in our lives, then quickly discard them as dangerous to our spiritual well-being. Then, when we are faithful to follow his Word, he is free to lend supernatural assistance.

The Family: Rebuilding the family unit in the destructive wake of incest is low on the priority list of some counselors and treatment programs. Their philosophy is, "Why bother? They're better off without him." There are several problems with such an attitude. First, if the molester is not treated and reunited with his family, he may slip through the system and find another family to victimize. Second, if the family breaks up, it often serves to reinforce the guilt already felt by the victim. Also, the victim may still love the molester, and depriving her of any hope for his return may be more of a punishment for her than for him. And finally, it is clear that God places a lot of value on the maintenance of the family unit. Consequently, helping the incest family survive intact should be a priority for Christians concerned with treating this problem. But no chances should be taken with the safety of the victim or the other children in the family. On the contrary, for reasons already discussed, the molester should be considered at all times during treatment to be a danger to these children. With proper precautions and a lot of effort, however, a family can be effectively treated while the victim's safety is assured.

Once a family has entered the treatment program and the mother-daughter bond has been established, it will be necessary to redefine family roles to conform more closely to those in a normal family. If the victim has taken the role of mother within the family unit, she will need to be gently but firmly directed toward the role of a dependent child. In turn, her mother will need to learn how to protect her children and to resume her role as a responsible parent.

If the role reversal in existence during the molestation has been established for any length of time, the transition back to appropriate roles may be difficult for both mother and daughter. It is sometimes hard for these girls to give up the power and control within the family they became used to, and their mothers are often hesitant to re-enter the threatening world of responsible parenthood. A lot of emotional support and practical advice will be needed to help these families through their readjustment period.

The incest family is usually so fragmented by the time abuse is discovered that treating the family as a unit is not practical until its members have received treatment separately. Issues needing resolution in these families can be quite complicated. It is therefore very helpful for the family to be involved in a treatment program such as Parents United, which has a great deal of experience and success in salvaging the family.

It will encourage you to know that some of the most well-adjusted and healthy families are those which have endured the trauma of incest and have completed their treatment with a determination to survive as a family. The supportive relationships and open communication seen in such families is truly worth the necessary effort.

The Molester: Last on the treatment priority list in the incest family is the molester. The feelings expressed by people when they discuss the topic of child molesters are understandable. Having made many public presentations on child sexual abuse, I am accustomed to hearing the less than merciful suggestions people often make on treatment of the molester, the most common being capital punishment and castration. But as much as I might occasionally be tempted to endorse such drastic measures, I also realize that this subject is much too complicated for so simple a solution. As there is more than one category of child molester, proper treatment for one may not be appropriate for another.

For the sake of our discussion on treatment, a few simple definitions may be useful, although definitions and terminology in this field often differ from expert to expert—even in professional literature. This may be due to the fact that child sexual abuse is a relatively new field of study. But in order not to confuse the issue, I will attempt to simplify the subject by employing common terms that may not be technically accurate.

Pedophilia is defined basically as a sexual perversion in which children are the preferred sexual object. The term *pedophile* is used to describe a molester who falls within that category. It is the pedophile who has been the most common subject of media coverage. The true pedophile is a predatory individual who premeditates his crimes and usually molests children outside his own family. These are the individuals parents usually have in mind when warning their children to beware of strangers, even though they seldom fit the hat-and-trenchcoat image portrayed by society.

The other main category of child molester is the *regressed molester*. The regressed molester is not predatory and generally confines his activities to members of his own family. This is the category into which the incestuous abuser falls, and only recently have such molesters been considered by the public when discussing child sexual abuse.

As far as treatment is concerned, our discussion will be confined to the regressed molester. The treatment of the true pedophile is usually not the concern of those to whom this book is addressed. In addition, the concensus among professionals is that the pedophile responds poorly to treatment of any kind. The regressed molester, on the other hand, has been shown to respond very well to treatment—as long as certain guidelines are followed.

It is easy to dismiss even the regressed molester as not worth saving. However, before we let our righteous indignation get the best of us, there are a few things we need to consider. We should remember that the regressed molester has usually himself been the victim of sexual abuse as a child. When does the victim stop being a victim and become a molester? I realize that once a person has chosen to violate the sexual rights of another person, he has committed a moral and legal crime, and that our prime consideration must be for the victim. However, I also believe that the molester should be treated whenever it is possible to do so without endangering the other family members. We might do well to remember Christ's admonition to the Pharisees in Matthew 9:13. He suggested that they learn what was meant by the statement "I desire mercy, and not sacrifice." And, for our own sakes, Christians should remember that "judgment is without mercy to one who has shown no mercy; yet mercy triumphs over judgment" (James 2:13).

The first subject to discuss when considering the treatment of molesters is how to decide which ones are suitable for the treatment programs we have been talking about. Since pedophiles have been shown to respond poorly to any form of therapy, it seems reasonable to consider them inappropriate for such community-based treatment. Therefore, by identifying the pedophile and eliminating him from treatment consideration, we can concentrate our efforts on those offenders who are more likely to benefit from counseling. There are a number of different factors that have proven helpful in identifying the true pedophile. Molesters who display any of the following characteristics or behaviors are likely to be suitable only for in-patient treatment programs, such as those found in prisons or mental institutions.

Contraindications to Community Treatment
(*Characteristics of the Pedophile*)

1. The use of violence during an offense
2. The use of sadism during an offense
3. Evidence of gross perversion during an offense
4. Exclusive sexual orientation toward children (seldom, if ever, has sexual relationships with other adults)
5. Offenses are predatory (molester seeks out or stalks victims)
6. Record of even minor sexual offenses
7. Record of serious criminal offenses
8. Molester refuses to admit guilt or shows no remorse or desire to change
9. Molester's primary targets are male children
10. Indications that sexual orientation toward children began during adolescence

Most molesters who have become involved in incestuous relationships are appropriate candidates for community-based treatment programs. But even if a molester is determined to be suitable for such a program, certain safeguards must be taken to assure that treatment at least has a chance of being effective. First, experience has shown that molesters do not remain in treatment unless they are coerced into doing so. Consequently, legal sanctions are usually necessary to assure the molester's attendance and participation in counseling. Many professional counselors find it hard to believe that a client can receive any benefit from a program he is forced to attend, but treatment progress is entirely possible under such circumstances.

Standard forms of introspective therapy, such as Freudian psychoanalysis, are seldom effective with molesters. Such traditional therapy methods are based on the idea that an individual is seeking help voluntarily and is willing to confide completely in the therapist. It is also assumed in such instances that the client wants to change the problem behavior. None of this is true of the molester. He very seldom seeks help voluntarily, and even when he does, it is unlikely that he will reveal the full extent of his problems and activities.

The molester is usually a master of manipulation. These individuals are exquisitely sensitive to power and authority. While they may be domineering beasts in their own homes, they often appear meek and pathetic in the presence of someone with greater social status, such as a therapist. Through the use of denial, rationalization, or feigned cooperation, the molester is often able to enlist the therapist as his protector and champion.

Because of such factors, the average family counselor is not prepared to deal with child molesters. Specialized sexual abuse treatment programs are thus the best treatment resource for incest offenders.

Therapy groups available through child sexual abuse treatment programs are especially effective in treating the incestuous molester. While he may be able to dance his way around some untrained counselors, it is a different matter altogether when the molester is facing a group of his peers. Other molesters who have already worked through their denial and rationalization are well qualified to confront new group members. When such groups are properly supervised by trained professionals, they can be extremely helpful in getting the offender to accept responsibility for his actions and the damage he has done. They also provide emotional support for the molester and reinforce proper attitudes through peer pressure. Many offenders even choose to continue attending these groups long after they are released from that requirement so that they can help other molesters and continue to receive help themselves.

As encouraging as the molester's progress may be in group therapy, there must always be a sense of caution in dealing with these men. If a molester seems unable to understand the feelings of his victim or accepts only partial responsibility for his actions, it would be dangerous to consider reuniting the family. The decision to reunite the incest family must never be based simply on the molester's apparent progress in counseling. The first criterion for such a decision is a feeling on the part of the victim that her mother is finally able and willing to protect her from further molestation. If the mother also feels strong enough to support her daughter and is not still acting jealous or suspicious of her, it may be safe to return the molester to the home—but such progress takes a lot of time.

Even when the family is reunited, the safety of the victim or her siblings should never be left to the internal controls of the molester. It must always be assumed, for the protection of all concerned, that the molester will attempt to resume his abusive behavior once the family is back together. Thus, protective measures should be taken accordingly. This attitude may seem harsh and unforgiving to the person not familiar with such cases, but it is completely justified, as the strength of this compulsion dictates extreme caution.

Before leaving the subject of molesters, we should deal quickly with the problem of adolescent sexual offenders. Recent findings indicate that sexual abuse of younger children by adolescent offenders is a very common problem in our society. Unfortunately, it is often dismissed as being sexual experimentation or the failure of a teenager to control his strong new sexual impulses. It may be that much of the sexual behavior displayed by teens is harmless. It may also be that some of that behavior indicates the beginning of a serious sexual adjustment problem.

Current research is showing that adults who molest children often began their abusive behavior during adolescence. This is especially true in the more serious forms of pedophilia. The problem is how to determine which behaviors on the part of an adolescent are indicative of serious sexual problems. In reviewing the literature on this subject and talking with people who specialize in treating adolescent offenders, I have developed a list of warning signals that might prove useful in this area. While the indicators listed below are not conclusive in themselves, the existence of even one is sufficient cause to warrant further evaluation.

Indicators of Serious Sexual Adjustment Problems in Adolescents

1. Genital exposure allowing a clear view (does not include streaking, mooning, peeping, or exhibiting in groups of two or more)
2. Solitary sexual activity (prowling or peeping while alone)
3. Masturbation or high sexual excitement during the act
4. Age discrepancy (subject of activity considerably older or younger)
5. Activity involves ritualism, sadism, or bondage
6. Use of threats, coercion, entrapment, or force
7. Activity is embarrassing or degrading to the victim
8. Abuser is pleased by or indifferent to the victim's reaction
9. Activity is sexually unconventional or seems to have a symbolic meaning
10. Activity is the exclusive means of achieving sexual pleasure
11. Activity appears to be a compulsion (repeated often)
12. Victim is a family member or a total stranger
13. Victim is particularly vulnerable (retarded, handicapped, or otherwise unable to protect herself)
14. Activity occurs during burglary or break-in
15. Abuser displays increasing aggression in sexual behavior
16. Abuser has a history of adjustment problems in home, school, or community
17. Abuser has an extremely unstable home environment

I wish I could tell you that treatment for adolescents displaying such behaviors is readily available throughout the nation. Unfortunately, such is not the case. In fact, there are few areas that have treatment programs for juvenile offenders. This may change within the next few years as experts see the potential for preventing future sexual abuse by treating young offenders. But such changes come slowly. Meanwhile, concerned adults should contact local child sexual abuse treatment programs to find out what treatment resources are available.

Treatment Issues

In considering the treatment of child sexual abuse, several issues arise which should be dealt with before moving on to the important subject of prevention. The first issue deals with the Christian's use of treatment programs which are based on humanistic philosophy. Some well-known programs boast of the fact that humanism is the foundation of their treatment. Considering the fact that humanism denies many of the beliefs held by Christians, it is easy to understand why some people are hesitant to take part in such programs.

It has been my personal experience, however, that humanism does not play a major role in most of these treatment programs. And, where it does come up, the average Christian usually has little trouble filtering what is said through his or her own belief system. The main area in which humanism affects these programs is in their attitudes toward forgiveness, anger, and hatred. Humanistic philosophy does not encourage a victim to forgive her abuser or resolve and discard her anger unless she herself considers such actions to be beneficial. The idea of forgiveness for its own sake or because God tells us to forgive is contrary to a philosophy which denies that moral values can be established supernaturally.

The unfortunate fact is that treatment programs claiming a humanistic orientation are often the only programs available to incest families. And because treatment is so critically important for these families, it may be necessary for the Christian to refer to or use such programs until suitable alternatives are developed. It is entirely possible for Christians to benefit from these programs if they temper what is said with the Word of God and determine to add forgiveness and other spiritual values to their own treatment goals.

Another treatment issue that deserves some consideration is the question of homosexuality. As explained previously, victims of sexual abuse—both male and female—are sometimes influenced by their victimization to develop a homosexual orientation. Most professionals in the field of child sexual abuse do not even concern themselves with this problem. The attitude seems to be that since homosexuality is so widely accepted in modern society and the victim has a free choice in such matters, any inclination in that direction should not be a reason for concern—let alone a target for treatment.

The Christian counselor, however, should have a different attitude toward this problem. First of all, such a homosexual orientation often grows out of the sexual abuse and should not be considered a totally free choice by the victim. Second, the behavior that results from such a sexual orientation is scripturally indefensible, as was pointed out earlier in this book. Therefore, it is important from a Christian perspective that this problem be considered when treating victims of child sexual abuse.

The final issue I would like to discuss in this chapter is the question of diversion versus punishment of incest molesters. Programs that treat incest families generally fall into two categories when it comes to their philosophies on punishment of the molester. Those in the first category advocate the diversion of the molester from the criminal justice system prior to trial in exchange for his completion of a treatment program. Most such programs provide for criminal prosecution of the molester if he does not live up to his agreement. Those in favor of diversion point out that the molester's desire to avoid a criminal record is a strong incentive for cooperation. In addition, such an arrangement usually spares the victim the trauma of a courtroom appearance during the criminal proceedings.

The second category is made up of those programs which advocate punishment of the molester as part of the treatment process. They generally insist that the molester either be in the criminal justice system or already convicted and sentenced before he begin his participation in counseling. Attendance in the treatment program is generally part of the molester's sentence or terms of probation. These men often receive a light sentence or no sentence at all under the condition that they complete the prescribed counseling. Advocates of this model stress that conviction and punishment serve to clearly identify the molester as the responsible party, thus relieving some of the victim's false feelings of guilt. It also allows for easier identification of the molester if he should complete the program, move to another area, and repeat his offense. This model has the added advantage of being easier to sell to the public at large because it advocates punishment of the molester, even if that punishment is really only symbolic.

Both types of programs have advantages and disadvantages; either can be extremely effective if properly supported by the community in which it operates. What is most important is that pressure be exerted on both the family and the molester to attend whatever counseling is necessary in order to resolve the problem and prevent further abuse. Incest families are often extremely resistive to intervention—especially the molesters. Programs developed for treatment must take this fact into consideration if they are to be effective in healing these families.

CHAPTER ELEVEN

An Ounce of Prevention

Up to this point, we have been considering the terrible consequences of child sexual abuse and the difficulties of recognizing and treating this problem. Now we will deal with a subject of hope. Prevention offers us the opportunity to take the offensive against sexual abuse rather than waiting in fear and picking up the pieces after the blow has been struck.

The concept of prevention has been slow in developing within our society. Basically, we are a treatment-oriented nation, more concerned with healing than with planning and prevention. Even in the field of medicine, our emphasis has been on repair and dramatic new treatment procedures rather than what can be done to prevent medical problems in the first place. We often fail to see the need for action until after we've experienced the pain. This tendency also seems to have affected our thinking toward child sexual abuse. Afraid to face the possibility that such a terrible calamity could overtake *our* children, we often choose to ignore the danger while we hope for the best. And because we don't have much faith in the idea of prevention in general, we doubt if the results will be worth the necessary effort anyway.

We need to wake up to the fact that it is entirely possible to prevent much of the sexual abuse taking place within our nation today. By following certain guidelines, parents can greatly reduce the chances of their children being sexually victimized. And, because of the dynamics of sexual abuse, by preventing the abuse of children in this generation we are also

137

preventing the abuse of children in the next generation. Thus, prevention proves to be an excellent investment in the future of our children, one which has the potential for paying tremendous dividends.

There are basically three categories of prevention—primary, secondary, and tertiary. The aim of *primary prevention* is to stop an event or series of events from happening in the first place. In the case of sexual abuse, primary prevention can be accomplished through the education of caretakers, potential victims, and even potential molesters. Primary prevention methods not only help stop acts of sexual abuse but have the added benefit of improving communication between children and adults.

Secondary prevention involves early detection and intervention in cases where sexual abuse has already occurred. When this problem is detected soon after onset, intervention and treatment are usually more effective and further episodes of molestation can often be prevented. Secondary prevention is accomplished mainly through the education of adults who are in a position to observe indicators of sexual abuse in children. This includes not only parents but also doctors, teachers, pastors, counselors, and any other individuals who come in contact with children.

Tertiary prevention consists mainly of therapy aimed at the victim of long-term sexual abuse and her family. The purpose of tertiary prevention is to minimize the emotional damage done to the victim and her family and, in so doing, to lessen the likelihood of sexual abuse in the next generation. It is hoped that the intense counseling and emotional repair used in tertiary prevention will decrease in necessity as primary and secondary prevention methods become more effective.

In this chapter, we will be confining our discussion mainly to the topic of primary prevention, as most of the important issues and material relevant to secondary and tertiary prevention have already been discussed in previous chapters. Also, primary prevention of child sexual abuse is an extremely important subject that needs to be covered completely and specifically.

Knowledge Is Power

Before we get into specific methods of preventing child sexual abuse, it is important to know something about the molester and how he operates. After all, the molester is the reason for the precautions we are about to discuss. And the more we know about him, the more successful we can be in protecting our children.

The study of child molesters is a huge topic in itself, and many books have been written on the subject. However, rather than seeking to understand what motivates the molester or getting into a lengthy discussion on types and subtypes, I will attempt to give some basic information on the molester and how he operates.

As we stated in our last chapter, there are basically two categories of child molester: the true pedophile and the regressed molester. The incestuous abuser is considered a regressed molester, and the predatory offender who molests mainly unrelated children is categorized as a pedophile. Most of the material we have already covered to this point relates to the regressed or incestuous molester. The reader should therefore be fairly familiar with how the incestuous molester operates and have some idea of the preventive measures that are effective against him. Consequently, the material covered in this chapter will relate mainly to pedophilic offenders.

The pedophile is often a fine, upstanding member of the community. He may even be married and have children of his own, although marriage for the pedophile is usually a tool for gaining access to victims or establishing a respectable front in order to avoid suspicion. Nearly all pedophiles have very specific preferences in regard to the age, sex, and personality type of their victims. One pedophile may prefer girls ages four to seven who are quiet and shy, while another may have a completely different preference combination. Children outside these preference categories usually hold little interest for this type of molester.

Many authorities theorize that pedophiles prefer children as sexual partners because they are easily controlled and are not sexually or emotionally intimidating. Pedophiles generally have difficulty relating to other adults, especially on an intimate level, but with children they report feeling at ease and in control. Control is an important issue to pedophiles. Since many of them were molested as children, it may be that they are attempting to regain the sexual control they lost during their own victimization.

While it may be interesting to speculate on *why* the pedophile behaves as he does, the most important thing for us to remember is that these individuals molest thousands upon thousands of innocent children in this country every year. Only by knowing *how* they operate can we develop any kind of meaningful defense against their actions.

The techniques used by pedophiles to gain access to their victims and insure the secrecy of their actions fall into five basic categories: special secrets, special friendships, bribes, threats, and violence. The pedophile is usually a good judge of which technique will work with each child.

The *special secrets* technique is a favorite among pedophiles. It works most effectively with young children, since they usually lack the information necessary to judge what the molester is telling them. In these cases the molester involves a child in a secret sexual game that only the two of them are to know about. As the sexual content of these games increases, the child is reminded that if her parents found out about the special secret, they would not understand and might even be mad at her. Children should be taught from an early age that the only good secret is one that can be shared by at least three people.

The *special friendships* approach is usually aimed at a different group of children. These children are often chosen specifically because they appear to be lonely or unhappy. Pedophiles using this approach befriend lonely children, listen to their problems, spend time with them, and, in essence, become parent substitutes. Children from single-parent homes are particularly vulnerable to this approach. Sexual activities are often not initiated until a child is so emotionally attached to the molester that her need for continued attention outweighs any reservations she may have about the sexual aspects of the relationship.

Bribes are another tool used effectively by the pedophilic molester. This is where the stereotype of the stranger with a handful of candy originated. Bribes may take a number of different forms, including offers of candy, toys, money, or an opportunity to see and hold a kitten or puppy. Since no emotional relationship has been developed, this type of victim is much more likely to report the abuse than is the case with the special friendships approach. However, many children still do not report abuse in such situations because of false guilt and the fear of being punished if their parents found out.

Threats are commonly used by pedophiles to maintain secrecy. They may be mild threats of "your mother will be mad at you if you tell" or ominous threats against the child's life or the lives of her family members. Although often very effective in keeping the child quiet, threats sometimes backfire on the molester by causing emotional disturbances or nightmares that tip off an alert parent or caretaker.

The final tool used by pedophiles in the molestation of children is *violence*. Very few molesters resort to the use of violence since it is usually not necessary and most molesters prefer not to harm their victims physically. Dramatic cases involving extreme violence or the murder of a victim make up only a small fraction of child molestation incidents, although they grab most of the headlines.

Pornographic materials are often used in conjunction with the techniques just described. Pedophiles often use child pornography to lower the inhibitions of the potential victim. By showing a child pictures of other children engaged in sexual activities, the molester hopes to convince his victim that such behavior must be all right. If successful in his sales pitch, the pedophile may in turn photograph his new victim and blackmail her by threatening to show the pictures to her friends if she doesn't cooperate. The photographs themselves may be sold or traded to other pedophiles or kept in the molester's personal collection. Pornography plays an important role in causing and perpetuating child sexual abuse, especially in its more violent forms.

Space limitations prevent our going into any more detail on the pedophile and his behavior, but the information covered so far will help you understand the basis for the preventive measures we are about to discuss.

Educating Our Children

Although there are some practical precautions that parents can take to help prevent sexual abuse, by far the most important preventive measure is education. When children are properly educated in regard to this subject, the likelihood of sexual victimization is greatly reduced.

The purpose of education is to provide children with the information they need to make the correct decisions when confronted with potentially abusive situations. Contrary to the concern voiced by many parents, this can be accomplished without frightening children or destroying their trust in adults. When appropriate material is presented calmly as part of a child's safety education, there is no reason to believe that the child will become frightened or upset. In fact, it has been my experience that children handle information on sexual abuse much better than their parents.

Preventive education should begin while children are quite young. As soon as a child is able to carry on a conversation, parents can begin by identifying body parts and explaining to the child which parts are private and special. Even very young children are capable of understanding that their private parts are only to be touched by certain people and that they should not touch someone else's private parts if asked to do so. The longer a parent waits to educate a child, the more difficult it will be to begin—and the longer that child will be left unprotected.

It is also important that the education of children on this subject be conducted by both parents whenever possible. First of all, it is clear from such Scriptures as Ephesians 6:4 that the training and guidance of children is the responsibility of the father as well as the mother in the Christian home. In addition, children should hear from an adult male that it is acceptable for them to say "no" to another adult male's inappropriate behavior.

Fathers should also be involved in giving male children permission to seek help when they feel threatened rather than hesitating because they are boys and should be able to take care of themselves. Finally, in regard to preventing incest, it is much more difficult for a father or stepfather to sexually approach a child when he has been directly involved in teaching that child about sexual abuse.

Parents should warn children about sexual abuse the same way they warn them about the dangers of crossing the street or playing with matches. When presented correctly, these precautions become just another part of the child's safety education. But just as with any other area of safety education, training in sexual abuse prevention requires a lot of repetition. As every parent can testify, children seldom learn with just one lesson.

Even at this point, many parents reading this book may not be anxious to begin a preventive education program with their children. There are always questions of where to start, how to present the material, and how to be sure that everything is covered—not to mention the discomfort many parents feel in discussing such intimate matters with their children. Fortunately, there are excellent educational materials available to help simplify this task and make it more interesting to the children.

The *Little Ones Teaching Kit* is published in Canada and does an excellent job of providing the information children need on sexual abuse.[18] Their activity workbook is a well-presented booklet that uses art, Scripture verses, and discussion in the education process. The subject matter is tastefully presented yet specific enough to get the point across. Children learn how God made them as special individuals. They learn about their feelings, their five physical senses, and how God made girls and boys differently. They are also taught about "good touch," "bad touch," and when it is all right to say "no" to an adult. Each child has his or her own workbook in which that child can write, draw, and color.

Another excellent program written for children is the *Danger Zones* series, published by Word, Incorporated.[19] These colorfully illustrated books teach children how to recognize potential sexual abusers, physical abusers, and kidnappers, and instruct them how to respond if confronted with one of these situations. Like the *Little Ones* kit, the *Danger Zones* books teach children how they are special, and that they have the right to protect themselves from anyone who would try to hurt them. These books are designed to be read by children between the ages of six and twelve, but parents are encouraged to begin reading them to younger children to instill in them these safety principles.

Both programs also include teaching guides so parents can lead their children through the curriculum. I was so impressed by these materials that I am including order forms in the back of this book for your convenience. You should know that I do not receive any financial benefit from the sale of these programs.

For those of you who would like information on other educational programs and materials, a child sexual abuse prevention reading list is included in Appendix C. Most of the materials listed can be ordered through your local bookstore or directly from the programs themselves.

Many of the educational programs available are aimed at younger children. If your children are older, you may have to develop your own program by adapting the principles covered in this book to fit their needs. Fortunately, in many areas of the country, older children have an opportunity to participate in child sexual abuse prevention programs now being presented in elementary schools. However, many Christian parents are skeptical of secular programs and have concerns about how the material is being presented. But before you refuse permission for your child to attend such a program, you should first observe one of the presentations. Schools usually allow parents to review the material to be presented, talk to the presenters, or even see an actual presentation before the program begins. I have seen a number of these program formats and even helped develop one for our local school system. Most are extremely effective educational tools and are responsibly produced so that children will not be frightened or offended by the material.

Open Communication

The best preventive education available will be of little help to children who are unable to communicate with their parents. I am aware of several children who have gone through excellent prevention programs at school but did not report sexual abuse to their parents because they were convinced they would not be listened to. Also, children are hesitant to share information which they believe might hurt or upset their parents.

The best way for you to prevent the sexual victimization of your children is to develop open communication lines with them. This means taking time to listen and to share their concerns and experiences. If you have experienced abuse as a child, share that with your children. It will strengthen your relationship and let them know that it is all right to talk about such things. Remember, children can handle a lot more than you think they can.

Open communication not only helps prevent sexual abuse and improve parent-child relationships; it is also very helpful in reducing the emotional damage suffered if a child is sexually victimized. Clearly, communication is an essential element in the prevention and treatment of child sexual abuse and should be cultivated by the concerned parent.

Greener Pastures

One group of children seems to be more susceptible than any other to the advances of the pedophilic molester. That group consists of children not receiving sufficient emotional support at home. When parents are absent, too busy, or just plain not interested, their children become extremely vulnerable to sexual abuse.

Molesters often observe children for some time before deciding on a victim. They look for signs of parental indifference, depression, or loneliness in a child. Pedophiles are experts at capitalizing on the mistakes of parents by offering a child the attention and concern she doesn't get at home. One pedophile bragged that he could move into any community and molest hundreds of children in just a few months. His secret was attention. If a child wanted to talk when this individual was watching television, he would turn off the set and talk, giving that child his full attention. For communication like that, children are willing to put up with a lot. It's a sad state of affairs when parents have to take lessons on parenting from child molesters.

If children are having their emotional needs met at home, they are less likely to be tempted by the greener pastures offered by the pedophile. The investment of time and attention in children is one of the best preventive measures parents can take in the battle against child sexual abuse. And it can be just as emotionally rewarding for the parent as for the child.

Choosing Appropriate Caretakers

In one southern California city, seven teachers in a preschool were arrested and charged with more than two hundred counts of sexual abuse against children in their care. Similar stories on a smaller scale come from

Florida, New York, and across the nation. It's becoming unusual to pick up a newspaper without coming face to face with another sexual abuse scandal involving people who are hired to care for and protect children. Sexual abuse happens not only in large cities; in a small rural community in northern California, a day care center was recently closed down after the owner's teenage son was arrested and accused of molesting a number of the children.

It should be pointed out in the face of all this publicity that most child care providers are concerned, dedicated individuals with whom children are completely safe. But the fact is that there has been a tremendous increase in the demand for child care throughout the nation as married women enter the job market in increasing numbers. Unfortunately, regulations and enforcement provisions for day care centers have not kept pace with the child care boom. As the shortage of child care providers becomes acute, unlicensed caretakers open for business and parents who are desperate don't ask too many questions.

These developments have not gone unnoticed by pedophiles, who take full advantage of any lapse in the protection of children. There are actually books available in porno shops that provide pedophiles with specific information on how to find paid and volunteer positions that will give them access to children. The Bible doesn't talk about the wiles of the devil without good reason. Parents need to be alert to these dangers and act intelligently when choosing caretakers for their children.

While it is impossible for the concerned parent to cover all bases in choosing safe child care, there are some basic guidelines that will help reduce the risk of children being molested by their caretakers. Since day care providers seem to be a major topic of concern among parents recently, a quick review of the proper procedure for choosing a day care facility might be in order. In addition, I have provided some precautions regarding less structured child care arrangements.

Day Care Providers: The proper choice of a day care facility is a time-consuming and sometimes embarrassing task, but the peace of mind and added safety that result are well worth the extra effort. To do a good job of screening available day care facilities, you must set aside plenty of time for phone calls and visits. You may also have to ask some frank questions of the prospective care provider.

Your first step should be to call the agency in your area that is responsible for licensing child care facilities and get a list of licensed providers. If you do not know which agency to contact, call your local welfare department. They should be able to steer you in the right direction. Once you have a list of licensed providers and have eliminated those out of your geographic area, call each of the remaining providers and ask them the following questions:

1. Are you currently licensed?
2. How many children are presently in your program?
3. How many staff members do you have?
4. Do the children ever leave the facility? If so, where do they go and who takes them?
5. Are there any adult or adolescent males who supervise or have regular contact with the children? If so, who and in what capacity?
6. What is the age range of the children in your program?
7. Is there a list of clients that can be contacted as references?
8. When can I visit my child?
9. What are the training and experience levels of the different staff members?
10. What form of discipline is used in the facility?

The fact that a facility has been licensed is a fairly reliable indicator that there has been some kind of criminal record clearance for its employees. Staffing ratios are of little concern as far as sexual abuse is concerned but may indicate the level of care a child will receive. The minimum staffing ratio for day care should be one adult for every six children, and one adult for every four infants. Children of the caretaker should be counted when figuring these ratios.

Whether or not the children being cared for leave the facility is an important concern since much of the abuse discovered in day care centers has taken place away from the facilities themselves. Parents should make it clear to caretakers that their children are not to leave the facility at any time without specific permission, nor should they be released to anyone without parental consent. Such stipulations should be put in writing whenever possible.

In regard to male employees, I personally consider it important to determine whether any men or older male children have child care responsibilities or even regular contact with the children. It is true that females molest children as well, but statistically a child is much more likely to be molested by a male.

The only other question in this list that relates to sexual abuse is the one on visitation. The fact that a parent may show up at any time for an unannounced visit is a big deterrent to any plans for sexual abuse. A good child care facility should have no objection to a parental visit at any time without prior notice. This is one point on which the concerned parent should not be in the least flexible.

After choosing one or two facilities you feel the most comfortable with, visit those facilities before making your final decision. As you visit, ask yourself the following questions:

1. Are the children here involved? Are they enjoying themselves?
2. Do I feel comfortable here?
3. Does my child seem comfortable here?
4. Do the children relate well to the caretakers and seem to trust them?
5. Do the caretakers communicate with the children?
6. Are the caretakers patient with the children?
7. Do the caretakers motivate children with praise and encouragement or with orders and negative comments?
8. Is there enough room for play and rest?
9. Are there enough activities to hold the interest of the children?
10. Are there limits on the amount of time children can watch television?
11. Are there arrangements for medical emergencies?

There are many other questions you may wish to consider while visiting facilities, but those just listed will give you a general idea of the atmosphere in the facility and the attitude of the caretakers who will be responsible for your child. If you don't feel right about a facility or the individuals who work in it, trust your feelings and look elsewhere. Don't let yourself be pressured into making the wrong choice.

Once you have chosen a facility, the most important part of prevention begins. It is at this point that many parents relax and become content with the daily routine of dropping off and picking up their children. However, it is also at this point that the risks begin. After your child is enrolled in a day care program, you should make a habit of unannounced visits to the facility. Spend some time there and observe the interaction between your child and the caretakers. Talk to staff members about any concerns you have and don't be afraid to ask questions.

When relating to your child at home after placement, be sensitive to any changes in personality or behavior. Talk casually with your child about his or her new friends and their activities at the facility. Also, be aware of any changes in sleep patterns that may come about after your child begins the program. Some change is to be expected with initial placement, but things should stabilize as soon as your child is accustomed to the new people and routine.

If you have been faithful to educate your children in regard to sexual abuse and are sensitive to their behavior and comments while attending day care, you have taken important steps in protecting them from abuse. While there is no guarantee that any child is safe from sexual abuse in a day care or preschool setting, children whose parents have taken such precautions have been given an edge on safety.

Baby-sitters: While sexual abuse in day care centers has been receiving much publicity recently, it is actually more probable that a child will be molested at home by a baby-sitter. Baby-sitters have exclusive access to children for hours and, if they have the slightest inclination to initiate sexual activity, they could ask for no better opportunity. Parents may even inadvertently contribute to such a possibility by reminding their children to "be sure and do what you are told," as they leave for their evening out.

Unfortunately, there is no effective way to screen baby-sitters. The fact that a teenager is nice and well-behaved has little to do with his or her inclination to molest children. The best advice I can offer is that parents not allow men or adolescent boys to sit with their children. The differences in male and female sexual response covered in chapter 3 are important considerations that should not, under any circumstances, be ignored when deciding on a baby-sitter. This may sound a little paranoid but it is *much* better to be safe than to be sorry.

Clubs, Organizations, and Sports Activities: Many workers in this field often ask themselves if they are overreacting to the dangers of child sexual abuse because of their jobs or the fact that they are constantly in contact with people who neglect and abuse children. But it usually isn't long before another newspaper article or sexual abuse case convinces them otherwise. These are not isolated incidents or senseless attacks by deranged individuals. They are clever, premeditated crimes committed by people often considered to be beyond suspicion.

It is true that the great majority of adults who supervise children in scout groups, clubs, and youth sports activities are dedicated individuals who do not have the slightest intention of molesting children. But others are pedophiles, pure and simple, who have volunteered for such positions for the sole purpose of gaining unsuspected access to children.

Not long ago in a neighboring county a seventy-one-year-old scout-master was sentenced to eight years in prison for the molestation of two boys in his scout troop. Some of the incidents of molestation had reportedly occurred during official scout functions. Others had taken place at his home where he had invited the victims to stay overnight and work on scout projects. This individual, an active church member, confessed that six years prior to his conviction, he had been caught in the act of sodomizing a boy. He claimed that when he confessed to his pastor what he had done, the pastor reportedly told him he would not inform the authorities if the man would seek counseling. The molester never sought help for his problem and the whole episode was forgotten until he was caught again.

Reports of sexual abuse by recreation supervisors, youth league coaches, community volunteers, and other supervising adults are numerous and heartbreaking. What can parents do to prevent the victimization of their children as they participate in such programs? Probably the best solution to this problem is for the parents to become involved in these activities with their children.

Parents can volunteer their services as scout leaders, coaches, and activity supervisors. If that's out of the question, they can attend as many functions as possible. And, when unable even to attend, parents should find out when meetings or activities begin and end and see that their children do not arrive early or stay late. Offers of special outings or overnight trips for your children should be graciously declined unless the parent can go along. And, above all, parents should keep their communication with their children open and honest at all times.

There are some children's activities for which parents cannot take any concrete precautions against sexual abuse. When a child is on an outing with another family, at summer camp, or attending a slumber party, the real importance of preventive education becomes clear. Parents cannot and should not restrict their children from all outside activities for fear of sexual abuse. What they can do is find out more about the family or activity in question, pray for the safety of their children, and know that they did a good job of preventive education.

While the preventive measures we have been discussing in this chapter do provide some measures of safety for our children, they are far from foolproof. Such precautions alone are not enough. As Christian parents we need to pray for the safety of our children daily, remembering the admonition found in 1 Peter 5:8:

> Be sober, be vigilant; because your adversary the devil, as a roaring lion, walketh about, seeking whom he may devour (KJV).

CHAPTER TWELVE

Letters from the Heart

A Letter to Victims, Young and Old

Whether you are being sexually abused at this time or have escaped your abuser, I hope you realize after having read this book that you are not alone. Literally millions of individuals across this nation have experienced the same pain and confusion that you have. What happened is not your fault. The blame belongs totally to the adult who chose to take advantage of an innocent child.

If you are still being molested, please tell someone about it. What is happening to you will not stop unless you tell and keep telling until someone believes you. Adults who sexually abuse children do not stop until someone makes them stop, no matter what they promise. You may very much love the person who is hurting you but you must remember that he is sick and needs help. He cannot get that help unless you tell someone what is happening. Start by telling your mother. If she does not believe you or won't protect you, tell a teacher, a policeman, or someone else you trust.

If you are an adult who was molested as a child, memories of your victimization have likely plagued you for years. At times you may have succeeded in forgetting the emotional pain that resulted from your molestation only to have it return unexpectedly with someone's comment, the sight of a girl with her father, or something your husband has said or done. Until you talk about your past and deal with your feelings, you will continue to be victimized by them.

Remember, there is help available, not only from other people but from a loving God who desires to see you healed. It *is* possible to forgive the person who hurt you so terribly and to give up the anger and hatred that can destroy you from within. Knowledge and forgiveness will allow you to leave behind a painful past and look forward to a positive future.

For those of you who now have children of your own, it is important that you remember they are at high risk of being sexually abused. Because of this fact, extra care must be taken to protect them. Keep in mind that the same person who molested you will almost surely molest your children if given the opportunity. For the sake of your children, please review chapter 11 on prevention in order to remind yourself of this danger.

Finally, remember that you as an individual are valued and loved by the Creator of all things. God knew you before you were born (Ps. 139:13) and loved you so much that he sent his only Son to die for *you* (John 3:16). If God thinks that much of you, shouldn't you at least stop condemning yourself for something that wasn't even your fault? Jesus died for you not only that you might have eternal life but that you might receive healing now through his sacrifice (Isa. 53:5).

A Letter to Christian Parents

I wish it were possible to assure you that Christian parents have no need to be concerned about child sexual abuse, but such is not the case. This problem poses the same danger to your children that it does to children of the world. Therefore, concerned Christian parents have no choice but to prepare for the worst while they pray for the best.

Obviously it is better to prevent sexual abuse from occurring in the first place than to treat a child after the damage has been done. But effective prevention requires open communication between parents and children. Talk to your children! And, more importantly, listen to them! You will find that open communication will not only help protect your children from sexual abuse but will improve your overall relationship with them.

As you teach your children frankly and calmly about these dangers, remember that repetition is essential. Even though all concerned may grow weary of this subject, your persistence can prevent a lot of grief in the future. The problems of preventive training are nothing compared to those resulting from sexual abuse.

Unfortunately, even the best preventive methods are no guarantee against sexual abuse. It is therefore important that you also be alert to any sign that your children may have been abused. Please don't allow any hints to go unnoticed. Children are often just as uncomfortable with this subject as their parents, so be sensitive to what they may be trying to tell you indirectly.

If the unthinkable happens, it is absolutely essential that you believe and support your child regardless of any pressure to do otherwise. Without your acceptance and support, serious permanent damage will result. Put yourself in your child's place and imagine what it must have been like to experience sexual abuse. If you were molested yourself as a child, try and remember how you felt and treat your child as you wish you had been treated.

Also remember that no matter who the molester turns out to be, he is not to be trusted with your child. Never count on his honesty or self-control to prevent further abuse. And keep in mind that it only takes a few minutes to molest a child. Your children are counting on you for protection!

A Letter to the Molester

If you have molested a child and are reading this book, chances are very good that no one knows about your problem but you, your victim, and God. I hope the material presented has been helpful in making you aware of how your victim feels and the emotional damage your actions have caused.

You should no longer be able to convince yourself that what happened was the child's fault or that your behavior may somehow have been justified or even beneficial to your victim. On behalf of the many victims I have counseled, I assure you that there is nothing positive in what you have done.

You should also know, however, that you can go a long way toward correcting the damage you have done by taking responsibility for your actions and getting help for your problem. Chances are you were sexually abused yourself as a child and have suffered emotional damage as a result.

You are not the only one with this problem, and help is available—but *you* must be willing to take the first step.

Don't try to kid yourself that you can stop this behavior on your own. Perhaps you have already tried and failed. For your own sake as well as that of your victim, get help for your problem while it is still possible. By admitting your guilt, you can escape this terrible secret that has kept you, as well as your victim, in bondage for so long.

If you have been involved in an incestuous relationship, you should be aware that it is often possible to restore love and respect between molester and victim through proper treatment. But without treatment, it is unlikely that reconciliation will ever occur.

Should you decide, for whatever reason, to ignore your problem and continue your abusive behavior, you must understand that God will not hold you guiltless in this matter. I am convinced that his judgment will be sure and terrible for those who betray the innocence of children and refuse to repent of their actions. At the same time, he has promised to forgive *any* sin when repentance is genuine (1 John 1:9). It is my sincere hope that you will choose the path of repentance and reconciliation.

A Letter to Pastors and Other Christian Counselors

As we have seen in this book, the problems associated with child sexual abuse are complex and far-reaching. It will be up to you as a Christian helping professional to adapt the information presented to your own personal style of counseling as you work with families affected by this problem. However, there are a few points that need to be re-emphasized before we end our discussion.

First of all, it is extremely important to the victim of sexual abuse that counselors be aware of the danger of remolestation after sexual abuse is discovered. To accept the assurances of a molester or non-offending parent that sexual abuse will not continue is to place the victim in danger of further abuse. It should never be assumed that the molester is able to control his sexual feelings toward the victim or the victim's siblings, no matter how socially or emotionally stable he may appear.

I would also like to encourage those of you who work with incest families to adopt as a treatment priority the establishment of a mutually supportive relationship between the victim and her mother. Experience has shown that treatment is much more effective in families where such a bond has been established soon after the discovery of abuse. I have personally seen some beautiful mother-daughter relationships develop in families where this principle has been honored during treatment.

As pastor or counselor, you will play an important role in the healing of both the victim and her family. But in order to be effective, you must be well-informed and willing to confront the problem and the molester head-on while tempering your counsel with mercy and concern. In other words, you will need to be as wise as a serpent and as gentle as a dove (Matt. 10:16).

It is my prayer that God will strengthen you for the work ahead as you apply your knowledge to the task of helping the victims of child sexual abuse and their families. Take courage from the assurance that by treating sexual abuse in this generation you are preventing it in the next.

APPENDIX A

Following is a current list of child sexual abuse training programs funded by the U.S. Department of Health and Human Services National Center on Child Abuse and Neglect. To obtain information on the resources nearest you, contact the program which covers your area.

CAUSES
836 West Wellington Avenue
Chicago, IL 60657
(312) 472-6924

Illinois	Minnesota
Indiana	Missouri
Iowa	Nebraska
Kansas	Ohio
Michigan	Wisconsin

Institute for the Community
  as Extended Family
P.O. Box 952
San Jose, CA 95108
(408) 280-5055

California	Nevada
Hawaii	New Mexico

Sexual Assault Center
Harborview Medical Center
325 Ninth Avenue
Seattle, WA 98104
(206) 223-3047

Alaska	Oregon
Colorado	South Dakota
Idaho	Utah
Montana	Washington
North Dakota	Wyoming

Child and Family Services of Knox County
114 Dameron Avenue NW
Knoxville, TN 37917
(615) 524-2653

Alabama	Mississippi
Arizona	North Carolina
Arkansas	Oklahoma
Florida	South Carolina
Georgia	Tennessee
Kentucky	Texas
Louisiana	

The Joseph J. Peters Institute
112 South 16th Street
Philadelphia, PA 19102
(215) 568-3461

Connecticut	New York
Delaware	Pennsylvania
Maine	Rhode Island
Maryland	Vermont
Massachusetts	Virginia
New Hampshire	Washington, D.C.
New Jersey	

Child Sexual Abuse Treatment Programs
with Parents United Chapters in North America

Following is a current list of individuals and organizations to contact regarding child sexual abuse treatment resources. Your local welfare department or child protective services unit may also have valuable information available on treatment resources, or you may call the Parents United office in San Jose, California (408-280-5055).

ALASKA
Ray Clements, PhD
Parents United. Ste. B
303 E. 15th Terrace
Anchorage, AK 99501
(907) 276-6440

ARIZONA
Bisbee
Ron Newman, Exec. Dir.
Cochise Community
Counseling Services, Inc.
El Rancho Plaza #8
HWY 92
Bisbee, AZ 85603
(602) 432-5484

Casa Grande
Anne Horne, Coord.
Behavorial Health Agency
1919 North Turkell Road
Casa Grande, AZ 85222
Doug Miller, Dist. Mgr.
(602) 735-2351

Phoenix
Lee Fischer, Dir.
Suzanne Landig, Coord.
Parents United
of Maricopa Cty.
1521 S. Indian Bend
Tempe, AZ 85281
(602) 968-2918

Tucson
Donna Colbert
Parents United Coord.
Las Familias
5315 E. Broadway Ave.
Suite 204
Tucson, AZ 85711
(602) 747-1441

Yuma
Charlene L. Hicks
Children's Village
257 South Third Avenue
Yuma, AZ 85364
(602) 783-2394

CALIFORNIA
Alameda County
Emergency Response Unit
La Vista Unit 2
2300 Fairmont Dr.
San Leandro, CA 94578
(415) 483-9300

Butte County
Emmett Anderson, PhD
Lori Kuhns
Step II
Psychological Serv.
173 E. 4th Avenue
Chico, CA 95926
(916) 891-0674

Contra Costa County
John Morrow
Parents United Coord.
Child & Family
Therapy Center
1210 Alhambra
Martinez, CA 94553
(415) 229-4090

Humboldt County
Bruce E. Silvey, MA
Executive Director
Family Service Center
2841 "E" Street
Eureka, CA 95501
(707) 443-7358

Imperial County
Peggy Devoy
Imperial County
Child Abuse
Prevention Council
107 South 5th
Suite 224
El Centro, CA 92243
(619) 353-8300

Kern County
Trish Massa
Kern Co. Mental Health
1960 Flower Street
Bakersfield, CA 93305
(805) 861-2251

Los Angeles County
Antelope Valley
Sandy Devoe
Dept. of Public
Social Services
P. O. Box 922
Montebello, CA
90640–0922
(213) 727–4119

Los Angeles
Alfonso Garcia
Chief Coordinator,
Greater L.A. Area
P. O. Box 922
Montebello, CA
90640–0922
(213) 727–4080
(213) 727–4089

Long Beach
Carol Reed
Dept. of Public
Social Services
P. O. Box 922
Montebello, CA
90640–0922
(213) 727–4087

Los Angeles County—
Spanish Speaking
Salvador Perez
5427 East Whittier Blvd.
Los Angeles, CA 90022
(213) 727–4088

Monterey Park
Colleen Friend
Dept. of Public
Social Services
P. O. Box 922
Montebello, CA
90640–0922
(213) 727–4094

Pomona
Amaryllis Watkins
Dept. of Public
Social Services
P. O. Box 922
Montebello, CA
90640–0922
(213) 727–4112

Van Nuys
Mary Wilkinson
Dept. of Public
Social Services
P. O. Box 922
Montebello, CA
90640–0922
(213) 727–4091

UCLA
Susan Moan
Neuro Psych. Institute
750 Westwood Plaza
Los Angeles, CA 90024
(213) 825–0016

Marin County
Cheryl Barnes
P. O. Box 4013
San Rafael, CA 94903
(415) 499–0145

Mendocino County
Zena Marks
Mendocino Mental Health
564 South Dora Avenue
Ukiah, CA 95482
(707) 459–4638 M-T-F
(707) 463–4303 W-Th

Napa County
Chuck Liversedge
Parents United
Coord.
Marian Lodrigan
Mental Health
Out-Patient Services
2344 Old Sonoma Rd.
Napa, CA 94558
(707) 253–4306

Orange County
Rose Hassen, Coord.
Family Service Assoc.
17421 Irvine Blvd.
Tustin, CA 92680
(714) 838–7377

Riverside County
Banning
Elizabeth Murphy, LCSW
Parents United
Coordinator

San Gorgonio Child
Abuse Council, Inc.
P. O. Box 441
Banning, CA 92220
(714) 849–7858

Coachella Valley
John Shields
Family Counseling Svc.
82-380 Miles Avenue
Indio, CA 92201
(619) 347–2397

Riverside
Ray E. Liles
7177 Brockton
Suite 339
Riverside, CA 92506
(714) 682–7844

San Bernardino County
Barstow
Richard McDevitt
Coordinator
Karen Walker
Child Protective &
Placement Services
610 E. Main Street
Barstow, CA 92311
(619) 256-3546

San Bernardino
Verna Medrano
Parents United
Coordinator
David Myers, Director
Hiram Rivero-Toro, Dir.
Family Services
1669 North "E" Street
San Bernardino, CA 92405
(714) 886-6502

Morongo Basin
Irene Rocha
Chapter Coordinator
C.S.A.T.P.
1669 North "E" Street
San Bernardino, CA 92405
(714) 886–6502

Ontario
Margaret Walker
Chapter Coordinator

C.S.A.T.P.
1669 North "E" Street
San Bernardino, CA 92405
(714) 886-6502

Victorville
Carol Voll
Parents United Coord.
High Desert Chapter
Intake Office
14972 Circle Drive
Victorville, CA 92392
(619) 243-1556
(619) 243-1868

San Diego County
Chula Vista
L. C. Miccio-Fonseca, PhD
Senior Counselor
Parents United Coord.
272 Church Avenue
Suite 3
Chula Vista, CA 92010
(619) 281-3332

El Cajon
Lewis Ribner, PhD
Kearney Mese
Psychological Services
Suite 250
9455 Ridgehaven Ct.
San Diego, CA 92123
(619) 569-2055

Escondido
Skip Himelstein, MFCC
Parents United Coord.
Escondido Youth
Encounter
165 E. Lincoln Ave.
Escondido, CA 92026
(619) 747-6281

Mira Mesa
Patricia A. Holladay, PhD
The Center for Family
Development
9606 Tierra Grande
Suite 204
San Diego, CA 92126
(619) 695-2243

San Diego
Gary Vernon, PhD
Parents United Coord.
Steve Tess, PhD
Senior Counselor
Sarah Wachtler, LCSW
Senior Counselor
Department of
Social Services
6950 Levant Street
San Diego, CA 92111
(619) 560-3082

Oceanside
Julie Mennen, PhD
Senior Counselor
Parents United Coord.
Casa de Amparo
4070 Mission Avenue
Oceanside, CA 92068
(619) 757-1200
(619) 439-5544

San Joaquin County
Evelyn Crocitto, Coord.
Child Protective Services
Drawer F
Stockton, CA 95201
(209) 944-3345

San Mateo County
Kasandra Dills
Dept. of Health &
Welfare
225 W. 37th Avenue
San Mateo, CA 94033
(415) 573-2819

Bill Tiedeman
Family Service Agency
1870 El Camino Real
Burlingame, CA 94010
(415) 692-0555

Santa Barbara County
Santa Maria
Skip Purper
Youth and Family Center
225 E. Mill
Santa Maria, CA 93454
(805) 928-1707

Nancy Schindler-Migliori
Santa Barbara Mental
Health Service
207 S. Broadway
Santa Maria, CA 93454
(805) 925-0911

Santa Barbara
Lucille Calderon
Jeannette Green
Child Abuse Listening
Mediation Inc. (CALM)
339 Hotsprings Road
P. O. Box 718
Santa Barbara, CA 93108
(805) 682-1366
(805) 569-2255 hotline

Santa Clara County
Institute for the
Community
as Extended Family
(ICEF)
P.O. Box 952
San Jose, CA 95108
(408) 280-5055

South County
Lewis Pollard
South County Mental
Health
P. O. Box 668
80 Highland Avenue
San Martin, CA 95046
(408) 683-2344

Santa Cruz County
Vee Duvall
Parents United Coord.
532 Soquel Avenue
Santa Cruz, CA 95061
(408) 426-7322

Shasta County
Margaret Cantrell
Shasta County CSATP
620 Azalia
Redding, CA 96002
(916) 221-6875

Solano County
Charlene Steen,
Parents United Coord.
Mental Health
1408 Pennsylvania

Fairfield, CA 94533
(707) 429-6521

Sonoma County
Lorain Cardenas
DSS/CPS
P.O. Box 1539
Santa Rosa, CA 95402
(707) 527-2933
Martha Hyland
Teter Holbrook
(707) 527-2763

Stanislaus County
Deborah Johnson, PhD
Stanislaus County
Mental Health
1209 Woodrow Avenue
Suite A-3
Modesto, CA 95350
(209) 571-6104
(209) 529-6767 hotline

Tulare County
Shirley Panitz
Youth Service Bureau
P.O. Box 202
Tulare, CA 92374
(209) 688-2044

Tuolumne County
Jean Irwin
Parents United Coord.
Welfare Department
105 E. Hospital Road
Sonora, CA 95370
(209) 533-5752
(209) 533-5717

Ventura County
Herman Kagan, PhD
Program Director
Simi Valley
Mental Health
Children's Services
3150 Los Angeles Ave.
Simi Valley, CA 93065
(805) 584-4876

COLORADO
Boulder
Holly A. Smith
Boulder County
Sexual Abuse Team
Department of
Social Services
3400 N. Broadway
Boulder, CO 80302
(303) 441-1240

Glenwood Springs
Tracy Andus
Department of
Social Services
P. O. Box 580
Glenwood Springs, CO
81602
(303) 945-9191

DELAWARE
Bob Hall
Joan Kasses
Parents United Coord.
124 D Senatorial Drive
Wilmington, DE 19807
(302) 654-1102

FLORIDA
Alachua County
Alma Suckman
Parents United Coord.
CSATP
4300 S.W. 13th Street
Gainesville, FL 32608
(904) 374-5605

Miami
Cathy Lynch
Advocates for Sexually
Abused Children
1515 NW 7th St., Ste 213
Miami, FL 33125
(305) 547-7933

Palm Beach
William Harnell, Dir.
Family Services
Palm Beach Center for
Personal Growth

801 SE 6th Ave., Ste 102
Delray Beach, FL 33444
(305) 272-8500

James J. Arone, MSW
Child Protection Team
301 Broadway, Ste. 212
Riviera, FL 33404
(305) 863-1611

HAWAII
Jackie Baumhofer, Coord.
Kapiolani Children's
Medical Center
1319 Punahau Street
Honolulu, HI 96826
(808) 947-8511

Priscilla Minn, Coord.
Oahu Br. Admin.
1060 Bishop Street
5th Floor
Honolulu, HI 96813
(808) 548-5344

IDAHO
Boise
Patricia Heyrend, MSW
Dep. of Health &
Welfare, Region IV
P. O. Box 6213
Boise, ID 83707
(208) 338-7000

Pocatello
Tom Stoelting
Bannock Youth
Foundation
P.O. Box 4166
Pocatello, ID 83201
(208) 236-6082

ILLINOIS
Bolingbrook
Shirley Robinson
Child Sexual Abuse
Treatment and
Training Center
of Illinois, Inc.
345 Manor Court
Bolingbrook, IL 60439
(312) 739-0491

La Salle
Bill Kline
Mental Health Center
1000 E. Norris Drive
Ottawa, IL 61350
(815) 434-4727

Marion
Marjorie Kuechner
Illinois Dept. of Child
and Family
2209 W. Main
Marion, IL 62959
(618) 997-4371
(618) 997-4382 5-12 pm

Pontiac
Robert W. Kinas
Assoc. Exec. Director
Institute for
Human Resources
P. O. Box 768
Pontiac, IL 61764
(815) 844-6109

INDIANA
Bloomington
Rowena Lankford
Family Service Assoc.
of Monroe County
924 West 17th St., 10-A
Bloomington, IN 47401
(812) 339-0009

Mishawaka
Patricia Pugh
CSATP Coordinator
Family & Children's
Center, Inc.
1411 Lincoln Way West
Mishawaka, IN 46544
(219) 259-5666

Spencer
C. Jessica Hersch
So. Central Community
Mental Health Ctr. Inc
751 East Franklin
Spencer, IN 47460
(812) 829-4871

IOWA
Ames
Daisy McCartney
Child Safe Coordinator
713 S. Duff, Suite 2200
Ames, IA 50010
(515) 232-3335

Council Bluffs
Colleen Wettengal
Parents United Coord.
Domestic Violence Prog.
315 W. Pierce
Council Bluffs, IA 51501
(712) 328-3087

Dennis Tobin
Iowa DSS
12 Scott Street
Council Bluffs, IA 51501
(712) 328-5689

N. Central Iowa
Delphine Justin
Counseling Assoc. of
N. Central Iowa
520 South Pierce
Office 208
Mason City, IA 50401
(515) 423-9155

KANSAS
Debi Courtney
CSATP Coordinator
Johnson County
Mental Health
15580 South 169th
Olathe, KS 66062
(913) 782-2100

KENTUCKY
Carolyn Lindsey
Marriage & Family
Therapy Inc.
768 Barret Avenue
Louisville, KY 40204
(502) 561-3642

LOUISIANA
Pam Cohen
New Orleans Police Dept.

Child Abuse Unit
715 S. Broad, Rm 301A
New Orleans, LA 70119
(504) 586-3184

MAINE
Stephen P. Thomas
Community Counseling
Center
P.O. Box 4016
Portland, ME 04101
(207) 774-5727

MARYLAND
Baltimore
Mary Reagan
5735 New Holme Ave.
Baltimore, MD 21206
(301) 488-1789

Kensington
Linda Blick
1605 Concord St.
Suite 207
Kensington, MD 20895
(301) 949-3960

MASSACHUSETTS
Brockton
Terrence Flynn
Incest Specialists
Dept. of Soc. Services
143 Main Street
Brockton, MA 02401
(617) 584-0980

Gardner
Judith M. Linkous, Coord.
North Worcester County
Sexual Abuse
Treatment Program
Dept. of Social Services
196 Main Street
Gardner, MA 01440
(617) 632-9104

Salem
Phillip A. Mann
Mass. Society for the
Prevention of Cruelty
to Children

3 Hawthorne Blvd.
Salem, MA 01970
(617) 744-2910

Springfield
Kate DeCarr, Coord.
Sexual Abuse Self-Help
Program
Mass. Soc. for
Prevention of Cruelty
to Children
78 Maple Street
Springfield, MA 01103
(413) 734-4978

Worcester
Susan M. Getman
Regional Administrator
Greater Framingham Area
Mass. Soc. for the
Prevention of Cruelty
to Children
340 Main Street
Room 972
Worcester, MA 01608
(617) 753-2967

MICHIGAN
Bay City
Luke Stephan
Lutheran Child and
Family Service
P.O. Box B
522 N. Madison
Bay City, MI 48707
(517) 892-1539

Detroit
Barbara Reed
Parents Anonymous of
Michigan
1553 Woodward Ave.
Suite 541
Detroit, MI 48226
(313) 237-0947

Grand Rapids
Beatrice J. Christansen
Parents United Coord.
YWCA Child Sexual
Abuse Center

25 Sheldon Blvd., S.E.
Grand Rapids, MI 49503
(616) 459-4681

Midland
Sally Y. Ayres, Coord.
Midland-Gladwin Comm.
Mental Health Service
2620 W. Sugnet
Midland, MI 48640
(517) 631-2320

Pontiac
Debi Cain
Exec. Dir.
Haven
92 Whittemore
Pontiac, MI 48058
(313) 334-1204

MISSOURI
Kansas City
William J. Norton
The General Practice
of Psychology
108 East 117th St.
Kansas City, MO 64114
(816) 942-9532

St. Joseph
Ronald E. Hestand, MSW
Dir. Alpha Counseling
P.O. Box 484, Sta. F
St. Joseph, MO 64506
(816) 279-4116

MONTANA
L. G. Jarvis, PhD
Havre Clinic
P. O. Box 7348
Havre, MT 59501
(406) 265-7831
(406) 265-1349 7-9 pm

NEBRASKA
Kearney
Terry Scritchlow, PhD
South Central Comm.
Mental Health
3710 Central Avenue
Kearney, NE 68847
(308) 237-5951

Omaha
Toni Pastory
Parents United Coord.
State Director
Sona Building
5211 South 31st Street
Omaha, NE 68107
(402) 444-6839

Papillion
Rosalina Malone
Parents United Coord.
Sarpy County
Social Services
1209 Golden Gate Dr.
Papillion, NE 68046
(402) 339-4290

NEVADA
Las Vegas
Stuart Fredlund
State Welfare Div.
700 Belrose Street
Las Vegas, NV 89107
(702) 385-0133

Reno
Chris Marriot, Coord.
Washoe County
Social Services
Wells Ave. at 9th Street
P. O. Box 11130
Reno, NV 89502-0027
(702) 785-4861
Carol Humke
Department of
Social Services
(702) 785-5611

NEW JERSEY
Mt. Holly
Gail Tishman
N.J. Div of Youth &
Family Services
50 Rancocas Road
Mt. Holly, NJ 08060
(609) 267-7550

Ocean
Christine Hilligas, MA.
Coordinator

Monmouth County Sexual
Abuse Treatment and
Prevention (SATP)
2001 Bellmore Street
Ocean, NJ 07712
(201) 531-6060

Trenton
Edward Rasado
Family Growth Program
39 Clinton Avenue
P. O. Box 1423
Trenton, NJ 08607
(609) 394-5157

NEW MEXICO
Albuquerque
Beth Huddleston
P.O. Box 4620
Albuquerque, NM 87196
(505) 262-0581

Sante Fe
Rosalyn Malysiak
Robin Lackey
Exchange Club Parent
Assistance Center
839 Paseo de Peralta
Suite N
Santa Fe, NM 87501
(505) 982-8686

NEW YORK
Anne-Marie Eriksson
Incest Survivors Resource
Network International
15 Rutherford Place
New York, NY 10003
(516) 935-3031

NORTH DAKOTA
Bismarck
Mary Lee Steele
West Central Human
Service Center
600 S. 2nd Street
Bismarck, ND 58501
(701) 253-3090

Devils Lake
David G. Haugen
Lake Region Human

Service Center
Highway 2 West
Devils Lake, ND 58301
(701) 662-4943

Rolla
Chip Ammerman
Rolette County
Social Service Board
P. O. Box 519
Rolla, ND 58367
(701) 477-3141
(701) 477-5274

OHIO
Dayton
Zenith Lawrence
Administrative Dir.
Grace House
Sexual Abuse
Resource Center
Forest & Grand Avenues
Northminster Pres.
Church
Dayton, OH 45406
(513) 233-2781
(513) 879-5336 after 5 pm

Elyria
Patricia Manns-
Birmingham
Supervisor
Family Sexual Abuse Unit
Lorain County Children
Services
226 Middle Avenue
Room 302
Elyria, OH 44035
(216) 329-5340
(216) 774-5807

Mansfield
Constance N. Broody
V-P of STOP
Richland County
Stop, Inc.
220 Home Avenue
Mansfield, OH 44903
(419) 524-3662
Dave Krocker
(419) 755-5556

OKLAHOMA
Oklahoma City
Cheryl A. Wilson
Sunbeam Family
Services Inc.
616 Northwest 21st
Oklahoma City, OK
73112
(405) 528-7721

Tulsa
Gemma Voss
Family & Children's SVC
650 S. Peoria St.
Tulsa, OK 75120
(918) 587-9471

OREGON
Grants Pass
Phil Backus
P.O. Box 189
Grants Pass, OR 97526
(503) 474-3120

Hillsboro
Pat McGrath
Children's Services
1665 SE Enterprise Cir.
Hillsboro, OR 97123
(503) 648-8951

Ontario
Lucy Hutchins
CSD
P.O. Box 927
Ontario, OR 97914
(503) 889-9194

Portland
James P. Kenny
Interpersonal
Counseling Center
3706 S.E. 122nd
Portland, OR 97216
(503) 761-4239
P.O. Box 14708
Portland, OR 97214
(503) 236-7092

Roseburg
Howard Anderson·
District Attorney
Court House

Roseburg, OR 97470
(503) 672-3845

Stephen W. Voris
Corrections Division
Parole & Probation
1937 W. Harvard Blvd.
Roseburg, OR 97470
(503) 440-3373

Tillamook
Margaret K. Kellow
Corrections Division
2108 4th St.
Tillamook, OR 97141
(503) 842-8871

PENNSYLVANIA
Jim Hanneken
Parents United Coord.
429 Forbes Avenue
Suite 412
Pittsburgh, PA 15222
(412) 562-9440

RHODE ISLAND
E. Providence
Emma Pendleton
Bradley Hospital
1011 Memorial Parkway
E. Providence, RI 02915
(401) 434-3400 x106

Diane M. Petrella
Co-Director
East Side Center
173 Waterman Street
Providence, RI 02906
(401) 351-1501

Warwick
Kathleen Doherty-
Holmlund
Kent County
Mental Health Center
50 Health Lane
Warwick, RI 02886
(401) 738-4300
(401) 246-1127 6–9 pm

SOUTH CAROLINA
Sylvia Whiting
People Helpers
300 N. Cedar
Suite B-4
Summerville, SC
29483-6406
(803) 873-8483
(803) 871-9445 hotline

TENNESSEE
Jeannie M. Hill
Harriett Chon
Mental Health Center
511 Eighth St.
Clarksville, TN 37040
(615) 648-8216

TEXAS
Amarillo
Ann K. Ray
Potter-Randall County
Child Welfare
P.O. Box 3700
Amarillo, TX 79106
(806) 376-7214

Deer Park
Jerri L. Jones
Parents United Advisory
Board for East Harris Co
811 Center Street
P. O. Box 36
Deer Park, TX 77536
(713) 479-2831 x253

Ft. Worth
Deborah Moore
Family Alliance Center
1025 S. Jennings Ave.
Suite 103
Ft. Worth, TX 76104
(817) 877-3440

Houston
Liz Holmes
Family Service Center
4625 Lillian
Houston, TX 77007-5544
(713) 861-4849

San Antonio
John Dauer
Family Service Assoc.
230 Peredia Street
San Antonio, TX 78210
(512) 226-3391

UTAH
Logan
Roberta Hardy
Child & Family
Support Center
149 West 300 North
Logan, UT 84321
(801) 752-8880

Ogden
Duane Johnson
Family Support Center
622 23rd Street
Ogden, UT 84401
(801) 393-3113

Salt Lake City
Jeb Brown
Center for Family Dev.
3366 South 900E
Salt Lake City, UT 84106
(801) 466-8353

VIRGINIA
Fairfax
Miriam Royan
Fairfax County Child
Protective Services
4041 University Drive
Fairfax, VA 22030
(703) 385-8883

Fredericksburg
Dianne Dalby
15th District Juvenile &
Domestic Relations Court
Service Unit
601 Caroline Street
4th Floor
Fredericksburg, VA 22401
(703) 373-5429

Lynchburg
Geannitte Priddy
Parents United of
Central Virginia

C. Virginia Mental
Health Clinic
2524 Longhorn Road
Lynchburg, VA 24501
(804) 845-9048

Norfolk
Kathy Kralin
Child Abuse & Neglect
Coordinating Council
Carlton Terrace Bldg.
#518
920 S. Jefferson
Roanoke, VA 24016
(703) 344-3253

Suffolk
Martha L. Hodge
CPS Coordinator
Suffolk Dept. of
Social Services
P.O. Box 1818
Suffolk, VA 23434
(804) 539-0216

Virginia Beach
Fae Deaton
Parents United Coord.
1176 Pickette Road
Norfolk, VA 23501
(804) 623-3890

Dan Sandlin
Dominion
Psychological Assn.
1709 First Colonial Ct.
Virginia Beach, VA
23453
(804) 481-2298

WASHINGTON
Carol/F. Wayne Hough
Growth Counseling
N. 16831 Taramac Lane
Nine Mile Falls, WA
99026
(509) 928-5301
(509) 466-7921

WEST VIRGINIA
Jill Ragheb
Parents United Coord.
Family Services of
Kanawha Valley
1036 Quarrier Street
Suite 317
Charleston, WV 25301
(304) 344-9839

WISCONSIN
Kathy Staecker
Parental Stress Ctr.

1506 Madison Street
Madison, WI 53711
(608) 251-9464

CANADA
Alberta
Peggy Mayes
Caroline Anderson
Comm. Treatment for
Family Sexual Abuse
P.O. Box 1161, Sta. J
Calgary, Alberta
Canada
(403) 294-0767

Ontario
Oshawa
Grant Fair
Children's Aid Society
Box 321
Oshawa, Ontario
Canada L1V2P8
(416) 433-1553

Rexdale
Dr. Richard Berry
Thistletown Reg. Ctr.
51 Panarama Ct.
Rexdale, Ontario
Canada M9V4L8
(416) 741-1210

APPENDIX C

Sexual Abuse Prevention Materials

The Silent Children: A Parent's Guide to Prevention of Child Sexual Abuse by Linda T. Sanford (McGraw-Hill)
  A guide for parent-child dialogue.

No More Secrets: Protecting Your Child from Sexual Assault by Adams and Fay (Impact)
  Teaches children to prevent sexual advances and break the silence barrier.

What If I Say No! (M.H. Cap & Co., P.O. Box 3584, Bakersfield, CA 93385)
  An activity workbook for children.

Red Flag-Green Flag Program (Rape and Abuse Crisis Center, P.O. Box 1655, Fargo, ND 58107)
  Uses coloring books, a teacher's guide, and optional video tapes.

Speak Up, Say No! (Krause House, P.O. Box 880, Oregon City, OR 97045)
  Booklet uses cartoon characters to assist in educating children on sexual abuse.

He Told Me Not To Tell by Jennifer Fay (King County Rape Relief, Renton, WA)
  A guide for parents on the prevention and detection of sexual abuse.

My Feelings by Marcia Morgan (Equal Justice Consultants and Educational Products, Eugene, OR)
  Prevention coloring book for children aged 4–10.

How To Take The First Steps (Illusion Theater, Minneapolis, MN)
  How to get community and parental support for prevention programs.

Sexual Abuse Prevention Education: An Annotated Bibliography Kay Clark, Editor (Network Publications, Santa Cruz, CA)
  List of two hundred items for preventive education.

It's My Body by Lory Freeman (Parenting Press, Inc., Seattle, WA)
  Designed to teach young children how to resist uncomfortable touches.

Preventing Sexual Abuse: Activities and Strategies for Those Working with Children and Adolescents by Carol Plummer (Learning Publications, Inc., Holmes Beach, FL)
> Prevention curriculum guides for grades K–12.

Feeling Safe, Feeling Strong: How to Avoid Sexual Abuse and What to Do If It Happens to You by Susan Terkel and Janice Rench (Lerner Publications, Minneapolis, MN)
> Prevention materials designed for pre-adolescents and adolescents to read by themselves.

Child/Adult Prevention Principles Series Grades K–6 by Eric Berg (Network Publications, Santa Cruz, CA)
> A three-part series of small training booklets for children accompanied by guide booklets for adults, graduated by age. Three segments are K–2, grades 3 and 4, and grades 5 and 6.

A Better Safe Than Sorry Book by Sol and Judith Gordon (Ed-U Press, Inc., Fayetteville, NY)
> A guide to help parents talk to their children aged 3–9 about sexual abuse.

Sexual Abuse Prevention: A Study for Teenagers by Marie M. Fortune (United Church Press, New York, NY)
> A five-part study course for children aged 12–18.

NCPCA, Publishing Dept. (332 S. Michigan Ave., Suite 1250, Chicago, IL 60604–4357)
> NCPCA produces a number of different publications on the prevention of sexual abuse.

1. J. R. Conte and L. Berliner, "Sexual Abuse of Children: Implications for Practice," *Social Casework* 62 (1981): 601–606.
2. David Finkelhor, *Sexually Victimized Children* (New York: Free Press, 1979), 68.
3. Diana Russell, "The Incidence and Prevalence of Intrafamilial and Extrafamilial Sexual Abuse of Female Children," *Child Abuse and Neglect* 7 (1983); 133–146.
4. Edward P. Sarafino, "An Estimate of Nationwide Incidence of Sexual Offenses against Children," *Child Welfare* (February 1979)· 127–132.
5. Mary Rotzien, "Prevention of Incest, III: Survey of Pastors and Christian Counselors Concerning Incest." Presented at Christian Association for Psychological Studies Annual Convention in Dallas, 3 May 1984.
6. Gabriel V. Laury, "The Effects of Faulty Sleeping Arrangements on Children's Sexuality," *Human Sexuality* (December 1976): 6–17.
7. Report by the California Commission on Crime Control and Violence Prevention, *The Incidence and Prevalence of Intrafamilial and Extrafamilial Childhood Sexual Abuse* (1983), 173.
8. Ibid., 232.
9. American Psychiatric Association, *Diagnostic and Statistical Manual of Mental Disorders, Third Edition* (Washington, D.C.: APA, 1980) 236–238.
10. J. D. Herman, *Father-Daughter Incest* (Cambridge, MA: Harvard University Press, 1982), 104–105.
11. Finkelhor, *Sexually Victimized Children*, 68.
12. C. Rogers, "Sexual Victimization and the Courts: Empirical Findings." Presented at American Psychological Association Annual Convention in Montreal, September 1980.
13. Hennepin County District Attorney's Office, *Child Abuse Prevention Project Guidebook* (Minneapolis, MN, 1979).
14. U.S. Senate Committee on the Judiciary, *Protection of Children against Sexual Exploitation Act of 1977, Report on S.1585* (Washington, D.C.: U.S. Department Printing Office, 16 September 1977), 5.
15. D. Finkelhor, "Sexual Abuse of Boys: The Available Data," (1981), 30.
16. Conte and Berliner, "Sexual Abuse of Children," 603.
17. Katherine Edwards, *A House Divided* (Grand Rapids, MI: Zondervan Publishing House, 1984), 80–81.
18. Bill Katz and Lynn Heitritter, *A Little One's Teaching Kit* (Minneapolis: World-Wide Publications, 1983).
19. Joy Wilt Berry, *The Danger Zones Series: Abuse and Neglect, Kidnapping,* and *Sexual Abuse* (Waco, TX: Word, Inc., 1984).

Please send me _____ set(s) of *The Little One's Teaching Kit* at $10.00 each (price includes shipping and handling).

Name _____

Address _____

City _____ State _____ Zip Code _____

Send check or money order to: World-Wide Publications
1303 Hennepin Avenue
Minneapolis, MN   55403
attn: Grason Order Department

Please send me the following *Danger Zones* books at $7.82 for the first book and $6.85 for each additional book (price includes shipping and handling):

_____   *Abuse and Neglect*   # 0-8499-8224-3
_____   *Kidnapping*   # 0-8499-8223-5
_____   *Sexual Abuse*   # 0-8499-8222-7
_____   Also available for $10.77 is *A Parent's Guide to the Danger Zones*
0-8499-8225-1

Name _____

Address _____

City _____ State _____ Zip Code _____

Send check or money order to: Word Incorporated
P.O. Box 1790
Waco, TX   76796